Vision of Sai
Book 1

"*Do not belittle any religion or give pre-dominance to any single religion.*"

BABA

Vision of Sai
Book 1

Rita Bruce

SAMUEL WEISER, INC.

York Beach, Maine

First published in 1995 by
Samuel Weiser, Inc.
Box 612
York Beach, Maine 03910-0612

02 01 00 99 98 97 96 95
11 10 9 8 7 6 5 4 3 2 1

Library of Congress Cataloging-in-Publication Data
Bruce, Rita.
    Vision of Sai / Rita Bruce.
        p.   cm.
    Originally published: A. P., India : Sri Sathya Sai Books
and Publications Trust, c1991.
    Includes index.
    1. Sathya Sai Baba, 1926- .   I. Title.
BL1175.S385B78   1995
294.5'092--dc20   95-1937
                                        CIP

ISBN 0-87728-833-X
EB

Printed in the United States of America

The paper used in this publication meets the minimum requirements
of the American National Standard for Permanence of Paper for
Printed Library Materials Z39.48-1984.

Dedicated
To the Lotus Feet
of my Beloved
Sri Sathya Sai Baba

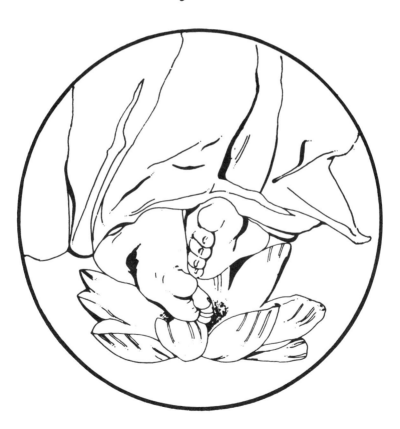

TABLE OF CONTENTS

ACKNOWLEDGMENTS

Sai Baba has taught me a fundamental lesson—that through His Love and Grace anything is possible, but my effort is needed. I never believed that I could write a book. Now my heart is full of gratitude to dear Sai, for he helped me achieve what my ego said could not be done.

Barbara Rogers, a devotee, helped me immensely with the earlier drafts of this book. Her enlightened feedback gave confidence, structure and form to my writing.

Sybil Primrose, also a devotee, came to my rescue at Prasanthi Nilayam after Sai told me to get the manuscript published. She was an example of selfless service, and gave countless hours to the finishing touches for this book.

Robert, my husband and spiritual partner, has been a principal player in our story. His encouragement and commitment to help in any way and at any time gave me wonderful and indispensable support. He is an integral part of this effort and an integral part of my life.

I ask Sai Baba to Bless these dear people with His Love and I humbly offer them my gratitude.

—Rita Bruce

BOOKS BY AND ABOUT SRI SATHYA SAI BABA

Available from:

Sathya Sai Book Center of America
305 West First Street
Tustin, CA 92680

Sri Sathya Sai Baba Books and Publications
Prasanthi Nilayam
Anantapur District
Andhra Pradesh 515134
India

PERIODICALS

Sanathana Sarathi
Prasanthi Nilayam P.O.
Anantapur District
Andhra Pradesh 515334
India

Sathya Sai Newsletters
1800 Easy Garvey Avenue
West Covina, CA 91791
U.S.A.

INTRODUCTION

An artist takes his brush and strokes until he has produced a painting, a picture on canvas. I, too, am trying to paint, a picture on the canvas of your mind through the medium of words. This picture is of Sai Baba– of unchanging everlasting Love and Light.

But how do you capture Sathya Sai Baba through the framework of language and explain Him with words? It seems impossible! And yet, if you open your mind and heart holding back the barriers of pre-conceived beliefs His Light of Truth will come from His Heart directly to your heart.....Heart to heart. I am simply a story teller, not a writer, the words of Wisdom in this book are those of Sri Sathya Sai Baba. Within these pages I tell you a story about my experiences with Sai Baba and how His example and words of profound wisdom have helped me to buffer the forces of negativity prevalent in our world, by teaching me what **REAL LOVE** means.

Living with Sai Baba and His teachings is not easy. But He is teaching me to have inner strength, to fight the war of good over evil, to fail and to understand your failing, to squirm and struggle with the ills of our society's life style and the results that have torn, worn and scarred my soul and in the end to succeed in reaching my goals.

He is teaching me to accept and change when possible the difficulties that occur in marriage, raising children, long term illness, a family history of drug abuse, and at the same time to accept and love myself and every being that touches my life.

I use many quotes from His Divine Discourses because within His teachings lies the proof of His identity. Many people hear of His Divinity and Miracles and say "Impossible!" They stop their investigation before it even starts. What's impossible for God?

Sai Baba tells us that His mission is to restore Truth, Righteousness, Peace, Love and Non-Violence because spiritual beliefs and right living were in jeopardy of being lost. Certainly we can all agree on the moral horror of our present society.

Logic would have us believe us that no human can correct the errors of our world. Then why is it so impossible to believe that God has come? The Christian community has been praying fervently for a second coming of Christ, then why is it so hard to believe that these prayers have been answered? Is it because our image, our concept of God, the Jesus form, is not present in Sai Baba? <u>Be careful.</u> Wasn't Jesus Christ crucified because he did not take the form that the Jewish community expected of God? Don't miss your precious opportunity by failing to study Sai's teachings. Many people assert that His discourses give a clear, simple and practical interpretation to complicated Scripture from every religion. These folk speak of an expanded understanding of old Truths, and a stirring or opening of love in their hearts. His words reach deep within us and strike a long unheard and yet familiar cord of wisdom. It re-sounds, a re-birth after a long term of silence.

I personally believe that when Sathya Sai Baba speaks to us there is an endless flow of Love Energy which we experience in countless ways. I believe that each sound that comes from His Voice is saturated with Love Energy, stored in the vibration of each letter. Locked deep within each Divine word is Truth and Love and as we read or hear our eyes and ears ignite each letter and release His Energy which is within the sound of each word. The sweetness of His Love comes from each word and melts our hearts. The purity and clarity in the Truth He speaks emits Light that sparks our inner vision, illuminates our intellect and liberates our egos.

Sathya Sai Baba repeatedly says, *"My Life Is My Message"*. He teaches us with words and His own example. Precepts without practice have no value. It is not only our responsibility to learn truth but to live it, He tells us.

He is an example of selfless Pure Love free from any trace of ego or desires. When you observe His flawless behavior, you too will recognize that no human could walk in His footsteps. The truth of His Divine Identity is clearly seen by His example of continuous giving, His equal love for all, every race, every religion, every culture, every status rich or poor, weak or strong, good or bad.....all are loved by Him equally. His love knows no bounds. His giving is limitless and timeless. His compassion is all forgiving. He is Omniscient, Omnipresent and Omnipotent.

You might ask, who am I to be a judge of this person who exhibits divine qualities? I have the same oneness that is within you that knows the difference between selflessness and selfishness, between love and hate.

Sometimes I am asked, why are you a devotee of Sai Baba? There are three major reasons: His Overwhelming Love, His Vision of Truth and Righteousness, and His Will that gives us the will power to transform, change our consciousness and ultimately our behavior.

Who do you know that has the power to heal the wounds, and scars of time and change one's life from 'I'-ness to 'One'-ness? You would answer, only God can do these things. I whole heartedly agree. It could only be God and all of these Divine qualities are in human form, the form of Sri Sathya Sai Baba, living in India.

The first part of that sentence is easy to accept, the difficulty is the latter. But remember.... **What we have never experienced, we can form no idea of.** So He tells us to come and experience Him, investigate the truth for ourselves. He welcomes us to bring our skepticism and doubts.

His extraordinary teaching power should not be overlooked. If for now His divinity escapes you, recognize and cognize Him as a masterful teacher, a Saint. Ask Him to reveal His Divine Identity to you. He can solve every problem great or small. Give Him a chance; don't miss His call.

Sai Baba says, His Mission is to re-establish Truth, Righteousness, Love, Peace and Non-Violence. The practical use of these four principles are defined in my life thus:

Living with Sai is Truth. When we have Truth, we are able to evolve faster because there is no hesitation caused by doubt.

Living with Sai is Righteousness. When we know what is right conduct we are able to discriminate between what is harmful and beneficial to others and ourself.

Living with Sai is Love. When we experience the pure un-conditional Love from Sai Baba, we are more giving and forgiving to ourselves and others.

Living with Sai is Peace. When we surrender, all desire to God; there is Peace. "I want Peace." Remove the "I Want", then Peace will flourish.

Living with Sai is Non-Violence. When we live and experience God's teachings we gain understanding. We understand that all of His creation is One, and if we injure any part of it we injure God.

The question remains:

"Who is this person in the orange robe with the halo of soft black hair?" Only you can search for this answer. He tells us that no-one even hears of His name unless it is His Will. So do not take another's word as your truth; seek and discover for yourself. Don't relinquish this golden opportunity and enter your grave, empty and lonely. **Go to Him** and fill your heart, till it overflows, with **DIVINE LOVE.**

Note to the reader: All the text that is quoted directly from Sai Baba is in *Italics.*

CALLING CARD

As I closed the door, and waved good - bye to the children it seemed like any other day. Usually I was awakened by the children calling me or fighting with each other. The first decision of the day was centered on "wardrobe". It never made any difference what clothes were clean and in the closet, there was always a problem. The mysterious item they wanted to wear was either dirty, ripped, worn last week, not fashionable, or gross. I got the same answers daily while offering suggestions.

The younger children were glued to the television watching cartoons while munching a bowl of dry cereal. What missed their mouth went to the floor. "Turn off the TV and get dressed," I yelled "or you'll miss the bus." If they did miss it then I was the family chauffeur.

According to priority, the daily questions continued.

What did they want for breakfast? Will they buy or bring lunch....if so what? Where was their homework? Then suddenly they would remember they had a permission slip to be filled out. "It must be in by today," they would say. And I would think, "what next?" My husband would call. "Rita, where's my shoes?" "Right where you left them last night, by your TV chair," I would reply. Why was it that I was the only adult in the house who could find anything?

This particular morning I heaved a sigh of relief but I was trembling like an earth quake. Standing there in my kitchen I began screaming as if I were mad. I yelled angrily at God, while I shook my finger at Him. "Where are you?" I screamed. "How could a God of love create a world of confusion and hate? If there is a God, what are you doing ? You don't know what love is.....nor do I. But when I find out, I'll tell you."

I was overcome with anger, and a burning desire to discover the truth. Did God exist? Is pure unconditional love I wondered just a theory or is it actually possible for man to achieve? My conscience told me that respect, thoughtfulness, consideration, and above all else selflessness was what I wanted to give and receive from others. And yet, if this was true, why did I see so little of these virtues in my own family, my husband and children?

I could more readily understand this lack in my children, but in marriage Robert and I entrusted to each other our vows to be loving and supportive in prosperity as well as adversity. Where had this love gone, or should I say "Did it ever exist in our character, or was it an illusion in our minds?"

The most severe pain I felt was watching Robert being sweet, kind and considerate to others. Where did it go when it was my turn to receive? Instead of the charm there would be harm. Instead of nice - ness there would be ice - ness. Everyday the words spoken were insults, digs, and put - downs.   I'm not letting myself off the hook, I did the very same to him which increased my feelings of guilt. I was so troubled, and felt so alone.

But my overwhelming desire was to correct this behavior and learn to give the type of love that I was taught existed as God. A love that is forgiving, accepting, kind, compassionate, understanding and most of all is aware and considerate of the needs of others. This urge surged through me with such intensity that I can still remember every detail of that experience, more than twenty years ago.

The paradox is that instead of me telling God "what love is" He's been teaching me. The lessons have been tough....tougher than I ever thought. And I have laughed many times at the audacity of my "ego". But the strength of that desire helped me to hang on, even when every fiber in my body wanted to "give-up".

Not only was my personal world a disaster but the national environment was as well. It was the malignant Sixties. All the American values and traditions were struggling for their very existence. People were robbed of the great leadership of John Kennedy, Robert Kennedy, and Martin Luther King whose lives were abruptly stopped by assassins' bullets.

It was the era of the Vietnam War and protesting; the fight for 'equal rights' and the blood-drenched peaceful demonstrations of the "Freedom Riders". Drugs jumped their inner - city boundaries and moved into the suburbs. The United States seemed to be injected with a "mania" serum. My own doorstep was no exception.

We were the typical middle - class American suburban family. My husband had a good job and we had a lovely new home, and four healthy children – all the ingredients that should create happiness, according to the commercials. One had only to "be there" to know that it was just another illusion.

I naively believed as so many movies portrayed, two people fall in love and live happily ever - after. I was so young, eighteen and very innocent. There were no classes to attend on Marriage. I was not prepared for the responsibility, the commitment, the lack of freedom, nor the inner sacrifice it took to love oneself and others in a manner that did not involve something in return, nor was Robert. We spent twelve years in ignorance hurting one another. All these rejections stacked up in our unconscious until there was no space left for any more.

The pain became so great that the force within erupted like a volcano bringing up the fiery emotional lava deep within the sub-conscious. Layers and layers of criticism, judging, and condemning, with angry feelings of bitterness and hurt, erupted and spilled out all around us. It seemed unstoppable!

We were so far apart that I wondered if it was even possible to build a bridge to span this vastness? The children were echoes of us yodeling the same sound of discontent. They were spoiled, selfish and continually fighting. It was the age of self-

4

expression; discipline was outdated. And my children excelled in self - expression!

I replaced the love that I sought and never received, with pleasing the senses by all sorts of activities with friends, shopping, entertaining, dining out, and sports. This type of pleasure satisfied me for a while but it was so temporary. As the years passed, the novelty of places, people and things wore thinner and thinner. My search became more intense, because my need for love and recognition increased. The pleasure I once received from outside interests held my attention less and less.

One desire after another peeled off as I replaced one for another. If I find a husband who loves me, I'll be happy. If I get children, I'll be happy. If I get my dream house, I'll be happy. If I get a Television, I'll be happy etc. The list was endless because one desire when met was quickly replaced with another...an endless stream.

I eventually realized how fortunate I was to be born in the United States because in a very short period of time I could acquire material possessions and quickly realize in a relatively short span of one life time that love, peace, and joy are not permanent when sought from the outside world. From this point of view it is understandable to say that "materialism led me to spiritualism."

One night, after the children had gone to bed, Robert and I had a verbal fight and in our anger we opened pandora's box. There was no way to retrieve the painful things we said to each other, but it made us both aware of how distant our relationship had become. It was painful beyond words.

A year earlier as our house was being built, a tornado hit it and destroyed everything. Our house had to be rebuilt. It never occurred to me until much later that our relationship also experienced a tornado in this new house. A psychological tornado.

Our inner home was hit by an emotional and mental storm. The contents were scattered and blown in all directions. To begin again floor by floor, room by room, item by item we had to examine carefully to see what contents were useful and usable; and those that were not, had to be picked up (seen) and thrown away. I had no idea how to rebuild our marriage nor repair our relationship with the children. All I could do at first was deal with the whirling wind of so many mixed emotions.

Almost simultaneously, I began hearing an inner voice and I thought my sanity was in jeopardy. Never had I experienced, nor could I relate to what was happening to me. I was having a spiritual awakening, but at that time I didn't know it. I had lived so much in my "outer state," I hardly knew that I had an "inner" one, until the emotional pain made me aware of it.

Since these different states of consciousness were so extraordinary I knew there was no possible way that I could have consciously created them. Today I would say that the Kundalini began to rise within me and I was not yet consciously ready for it. I was not a likely candidate for these experiences. My rational mind would say, "How could this happen to a Catholic mother who lived in the conservative Mid-West in the Sixties who spent the first ten years of her married life, pregnant and caring for her family? God must have made a mistake."

There was a part of me that knew within, I was being protected and guided as I lived through a maze of unknowns. But there were times that I felt unsure and I was frightened and so scared. One day when I awoke, I felt mild contractions in my head. As the day progressed, they increased in intensity and duration. They felt exactly like labor pains, only they were in my head, not my body. My rational mind said that maybe I was giving birth to my higher intelligence. They lasted all day and stopped as quickly as they began. There were also other times of beautiful spiritual experiences.

One day soon after I swore at God, I felt a beam of light coming down and entering my entire being. It extended and surrounded me creating a field of energy that is difficult to describe. Every atom in my body felt weightless, full of light, love and bliss. I called it Pure Love Energy. I felt that God gave me a taste of His Divine Glory, so I would always remember through the bad times what an exceptional goal I was working to achieve. It helped me to persevere.

A small portion of this light or energy stayed with me for three and a half years. It was an intense learning period, as we were learning from within that man not only needed to cleanse himself from all the negative programmed behavior he had, but also he had to understand how the four parts of a human operated. It was essential that these four parts were treated as equal and used in balance. We called them the "Four Energies" in man, and labelled them, the physical, the intellectual, the emotional, and the conscience.

One night I was awakened from my sleep by a voice

that I heard clearly. "Rita," it said, "close your eyes and watch. Nothing will harm you but you must see this." Then I had my first experience of an inner vision. I was shown a natural disaster happening exactly in the area where we lived. A colossal earthquake. I was told that this disaster was purifying man and the earth from the enormous pollution that had accumulated from waste and hate.

The magnitude of this disaster dazed me for years. I was told that Australia was a safe place to live and because of the vision and inner guidance we moved......to Australia. We sold our house and all of our possessions immediately and moved with our four children. Each one was allowed to bring only two suitcases. All other belongings we left to friends or sold. For three years we lived in Australia.

We were going to have a new beginning; this time working together to make a marriage of love. First we had to learn how to be loving. The achievement of this goal was not materialized instantly. The process has been a slow, steady, gradual change and we are still learning, but the results are worth the struggle.

My husband got a very good job, two weeks after we arrived in Australia. The children adjusted well. There was no disaster, in the U.S. But the move to Australia was extremely beneficial. It sheltered us from family and friends and allowed us to work freely on our behavioral problems without being disturbed by someone from our past.

We cut many cords while in Australia, not only physically but psychologically. The phrase used today is "Cutting Ties That Bind," which is the title of a book by Phyllis Krystal. We examined our relationship with our parents. We understood daily, more and more of our past programming. We visualized cutting the umbilical cord that connects mother and infant to separate us from our attachments. Instead of reacting automatically, we were able to look, understand, and slowly change ourselves. Even though insight was gained, application was slow.

Once in an inner vision, I was shown a place, a holy city where love and harmony ruled. Each person contributed their talent or skill, to this community. If you were a teacher, you taught, if a carpenter, you built etc. No money exchanged hands. Everyone served each other according to their ability and capacity. It was a peaceful and loving environment.

I was told that this is a new city being built by the Lamb, Jesus Christ, on earth today. After this vision, the experience was so real to me that I tried to find Him and when I told others about this vision they thought I was nuts! I soon learned to keep quiet.

Our stay in Australia was an intense learning period. Then as quickly as we were guided to move to Australia....we were also guided to move back to the U.S.A. again.

Our spiritual journey began in 1969 and not until 1976, did Sri Sathya Sai Baba identify Himself to us. In those seven years, my "higher-self" was preparing us to understand and accept the Spiritual wealth of the East.

Our story is about Sai Baba and His overwhelming Love. He has enriched our life, beyond belief. He has changed our consciousness and behavior immensely

9

and I can find no way to explain these spiritual transformations. But what I have written is true and as you read our story you will understand why I am so deeply grateful to Him for informing us of His identity. You will read why we became devotees and more importantly the reasons why we still are.

*　　*　　*　　*

Our physical relationship with Sai Baba began, one cold February morning in 1976, I was meditating trying to calm my mind. Then without any provocation, I heard a familiar voice – my inner voice, telling me with a clarity and wisdom beyond my conscious mind what the past six months had taught me.

For some unknown reason I found myself asking a series of questions, not particularly new questions, but old ones looking for absolute answers. "Who are you - my soul, Divine self, a teacher, friend?" All of these relationships I have experienced with this inner self, but was this my imagination or reality? I was still looking for absolute proof.

This time when I asked, I got this reply. "I am your teacher, and I will prove it to you this day." I listened intently. The voice continued, "I'll give you a big sign; go visit Pat and Brian this morning."

Pat and Brian are a young married couple whom I first met at our weekly discussion group for young adults. Being friends for several years I felt very comfortable calling them to inquire if they were free for a small visit that morning. They replied, "Yes, come." I never mentioned anything about my morning meditation.

As soon as I entered their living room, Brian asked, "How is your meditation, Rita?" I thought to myself, "He doesn't know about this mornings meditation, so why is he inquiring?" What a strange question to ask someone when you are just greeting them?

I answered very cautiously, "It's fine. Why do you ask?" "I have something for you and it will help your meditation," he responded.

Brian left the room and when he returned he was carrying a very large painting that he had just finished. I was surprised and puzzled with this unusual gift. Years later, I found out that it was a diagram or symbol of the chakras.

Brian told me that while he was painting this holy symbol, he felt that it was a link between **SAI BABA** and me. "Who is Sai Baba?", I asked. "He's a holy man in India," he replied, and pointed to His picture on the cover of a book on the table. It was a book written by Dr. Samuel Sandweiss, entitled "Sai Baba, The Holy Man and the Psychiatrist." I returned home with a new painting and a new book to read and stunned by the experience.

The next morning, I was sitting at the kitchen table, drinking my coffee. The children had just left for school. The inward dialogue continued. "How did you like my large sign?" I chuckled to myself, thinking it was literally a big sign! "It is my 'calling card'. I am Sai Baba." I thought what a strange remark.

Several days later when I started reading Sandweiss's book, I discovered that Sai Baba had materialized little calling cards with His picture and address on them and distributed them in an interview. He also referred to the gifts He creates for personal use like rings, Vibhutti, lockets etc., as My calling card's.

Repeatedly that day, I heard words of wisdom being recited to me like strains of poetry. It was sheer delight. I was mystified when I read Dr. Sandweiss's book and found these same spoken words there.

Sai said, *"Do not posit distance between you and me; do not interpose the formalities of the guru - friend relationship, or even the attitudinal distinctions of the God - devotee relationship, between you and me. I am neither guru nor God; I am you; you are I; that is the truth. There is no distinction. That which appears so is the delusion. You are waves; I am the ocean. Know this and be free, be divine."*

Next day, I read Dr. Sandweiss's book. I was captivated by the story of Sai Baba, a story about a holy man in India who has extraordinary superhuman qualities.

Dr. Sandweiss gives a detailed step - by - step account of his introduction to and investigation of Sai Baba, who was described to him as a person who could produce material objects at the command of His will. He could materialize a sacred ash from the palm of His hand called Vibhutti. This Vibhutti had properties that could heal people spiritually, physically, and mentally. Baba also knew the past, present, and future of those who came to see him. He not only cured the incurable, but even raised a man from the dead. He turned people's vision from the world to God. The stories of these miracles had the same familiar pattern as those told about Jesus Christ.

I thought "Is it possible for this person to be God in human form on earth ? Is this the 'One' I was told years ago to find?" As I read about Him all I could feel was Joy. His words touched my heart and I knew that what He said was true. His teachings renewed my faith in God, gave my life a new purpose, inspired me with hope for a world with love and created in me a feeling of security because He promised to restore our world to righteousness and prevent total destruction.

My search for absolute knowledge had ended. I knew that He would answer all my questions. My spiritual quest to find the meaning of love had ended - at His Lotus Feet.

He says, *"Prema or love is a much-misused word. Any positive response to an attraction is called love; any feeling of attachment, however trivial or transitory, is called Prema. We must certainly coin new words or set aside specific words to indicate the forms of love. The attachment of parents to their children or of the children to the parents must be called affection. The response to the attraction of sex is best described as fancy, fascination, or delusion – Moha. The feeling of kinship or comradeship evokes dearness. The pleasure one gets through a sense of possession, especially of material objects, can be known as satisfaction. The yearning to reach for the sublimity that lies inherent in Truth...this alone is entitled to be called by that holy word, Prema. For that is the sweetest, the most charming, the most satisfying possession of man. Love or prema is strong and steady enough to overleap all obstacles, confront with equanimity all changes of fortune, and defeat all attempts to delay or deviate. It does not judge one incident as good and another as bad; it does not ascribe them to different agencies. Just as the same sun causes both day and night, the same Divine Will causes joy and grief; so the devotee does not wince or exult when ill or well.*

"Love is a ceaseless flow of divine effulgence. Rishis call this love – atma. This atma which is full of love is shining in all hearts. Love, atma and heart are synonymous for God. For such pure love, there cannot be any difference based on mine and thine. This love is extremely selfless."

He also said that man is not the physical body. This is not our real - self but we believe it to be. He says that our **real** nature is Divine. He tells us that He is Divine and so are we, the only difference between us is that we don't know it. We don't realise it.....SELF-REALISATION!

"If you take one step toward me, I will take ten steps toward you. Remember that with every step, you are nearing God. And when you take one step towards Him, God takes ten towards you. There is no halting place in this pilgimage; it is one continuous journey, through day and night, through death and birth, through tomb and womb. When the road ends and the goal is gained, the pilgrim finds that he has travelled only from himself to himself, that the way was long and lonesome, but the God that led him unto himself was all the while in him, around him, and beside him! He himself was always Divine. His yearning to merge in God was but the sea calling the Ocean! Man loves because He is Love! He craves for melody and harmony. He seeks joy for He is Joy. He thirsts for God, for he is composed of God and cannot

exist without Him."

When I came to the following passage in "The Psychiatrist and The Holy Man," I sobbed like a baby.

"It was Christmas Day, 1972, and Baba was talking to a group of people." *"And the story says there was a star in the sky, which fell with a new light, and this led a few Tibetans and others to the place where the Savior was born. This story is read and taken on trust by man, though stars do not fall or even slide down so suddenly. What the story signifies is this: There was a huge aura of splendor illumining the sky over the village when Christ was born. This meant that He who was to overcome the darkness of evil and ignorance had taken birth, that He would spread the light of love in the heart of man and the councils of humanity. Appearances of splendor or of other signs of the era that has dawned are natural when incarnations happen on earth.*

"The aura of light was a sign that the darkness would be destroyed. A master arrives in answer to man's prayer: Thamaso maa jyothirgamaya (Lead us from darkness unto light).

"There is one point that I cannot but bring to your special notice today. At the time when Jesus was merging in the supreme principal of divinity, He communicated some news to his followers which has been interpreted in a variety of ways by commentators and those who relish the piling of writings on writings and meaning upon meaning, until it all swells up into a huge mess. The statement itself has been manipulated and tangled into a conundrum. The statement is simple:

15

"'*He who sent me among you will come again*', *and he pointed to a lamb. The lamb is merely a symbol, a sign. It stands for the voice: 'Ba-Ba'; the announcement was of the advent of Baba. 'His name will be Truth,' Christ declared. 'Sathya' means truth. 'He wears a robe of red, a blood-red robe.' (Here Baba pointed to the robe he was wearing.) 'He will be short, with a crown (of hair).' The lamb is the sign and symbol of love. Christ did not declare that He would come again; he said, "He who sent me will come again." That "Ba-Ba" is this Baba.*"

WHO IS SAI

DIVINE DISCOURSE

God is inscrutable. He cannot be realized in the outer objective world; He is in the very heart of every being. Gemstones have to be sought deep underground; they do not float in mid-air. Seek God in the depths of your self, not in tantalizing, kaleidoscopic nature. The body is granted to you for this high purpose, but you are now misusing it, like the person who cooked his daily food in the gem-studded gold vase that came into his hands as an heirloom.

Man extols God as omnipresent, omniscient and omnipotent, but he ignores His presence in himself! Of course, many venture to describe the attributes of God and proclaim Him to be such and such; but these are but their own guesses and the reflections of their own predilections

18

and preferences.

Who can affirm that God is this or thus? Who can affirm that God is not of this form or with this attribute? Each one can acquire from the vast expanse of the ocean only as much as can be contained in the vessel he carries to its shore. From that small quantity, he can grasp but little of that immensity.

Each religion defines God within the limits it demarcates and then claims to have grasped Him. Like the seven blind men who spoke of the elephant as a pillar, a fan, a rope or a wall, because they contacted but a part and could not comprehend the entire animal, so too, religions speak of a part and assert that their vision is full and total.

Each religion forgets that God is all forms and all names, all attributes and all assertions. The religion of humanity is the sum and substance of all these partial faiths; for there is only one religion and that is the religion of love. The various limbs of the elephant that seemed separate and distinct to the eyeless seekers of its truth were all fostered and activated by one single stream of blood. The various religions and faiths that feel separate and distinct are all fostered by a single stream of love.

The optical sense cannot visualize the truth. It gives only false and barren information. For example, there are many who observe my actions and start declaring that my nature is such and such. They are unable to gauge the sanctity, the majesty and the eternal reality that is me. The power of Sai is limitless; it manifests forever. All forms of "power" are resident in this Sai palm.

But, those who profess to have understood me–the scholars, the yogis, the pundits (scholars,), the jnanis (those who have spiritual knowledge)–all of them are aware only of the least important, the casual external manifestation of an infinitesimal part of that power: namely, the "miracles." They have not desired to contact the source of all power and all wisdom that is available here at Brindavan. They are satisfied when they secure a chance to exhibit their book-learning and parade their scholarship in Vedic lore, not realizing that the person from whom the Vedas emanated is in their midst, for their sake.

This has been the case in all ages. People may be very close (physically) to the Avatar, but they live out their lives unaware of their fortune, exaggerating the role of miracles, which are as trivial when compared to my glory and majesty as a mosquito is in size and strength to the elephant upon which it squats. Therefore, when you speak about these "miracles," I laugh within myself out of pity that you allow yourself so easily to lose the precious awareness of my reality. My power is immeasurable; my truth is inexplicable, unfathomable. I am announcing this about me for the need has arisen. But what I am doing now is only the gift of a "visiting card." Let me tell you that emphatic declarations of the Truth by avatars were made so clearly and so unmistakably only by Krishna. In spite of the declarations, you will notice in the career of the same Krishna that He underwent defeat in His efforts and endeavors on a few occasions, though you must also note that those defeats too were part of the drama which He had planned and which He Himself directed.

When many kings pleaded with Him to avert the war with the Kauravas (a family group in the famous Hindu epic, the Mahabharatha), He confessed that His mission to the Kaurava court for ensuring peace had "failed." But He had not willed that it should succeed. He had decided that the war would be waged. His mission was intended to publish the greed and iniquity of the Kauravas and to condemn them before the whole world.

But I must tell you that during this Sai Avatar, there is no place for even such "drama" with scenes of failures and defeats! What I will, must take place; what I plan must succeed. I am Truth and Truth has no need to hesitate or fear or bend.

"Willing" is superfluous for me, for my grace is ever available to devotees who have steady love and faith. Since I move among them, talking and singing, even intellectuals are unable to grasp my truth, my power, my glory or my real task as Avatar. I can solve any problem however knotty. I am beyond the reach of the most intensive inquiry and the most meticulous measurement. Only those who have recognized my love and experienced that love can assert that they have glimpsed my reality. For the path of love is the royal road that leads mankind to me.

Do not attempt to know me through the external eyes. When you go to a temple and stand before the image of God, you pray with closed eyes, don't you? Why? Because you feel that the inner eye of wisdom alone can reveal Him to you. Therefore, do not crave from me trivial material objects; but crave for ME, and you will be

21

rewarded. Not that you should not receive whatever objects I give as signs of grace out of the fullness of love. I shall tell you why I give these rings, talismans, rosaries, etc. It is to mark the bond between me and those to whom they are given. When calamity befalls them, the article comes to me in a flash and returns in a flash, taking from me the remedial grace of protection. That grace is available to all who call on me in any name or form, not merely to those who wear these gifts. Love is the bond that wins grace.

Consider the meaning of the name, Sai Baba. Sa means "Divine," ai or ayi means "Mother" and Baba means "Father". The name indicates the Divine Mother and Father. Your physical parents might cultivate love with a dose of selfishness, but this Sai Mother and Father showers affection or reprimands only for leading you towards victory in the struggle for self-realization.

For this Sai has come in order to achieve the supreme task of uniting as one family all of mankind through the bond of brotherhood; of affirming and illumining the atmic reality of each being in order to reveal the divine, which is the basis on which the entire cosmos rests; and of instructing all to recognize the common divine heritage that binds man to man, so that man can rid himself of the animal nature, and rise into the divinity which is his goal.

I am the embodiment of love; love is my instrument. There is no creature without love; the lowest loves itself at least. And itself is God. So, there are no atheists, though some might dislike Him or refuse Him, as malarial patients dislike sweets or diabetic patients refuse to have anything to do with sweets.

Those who preen themselves as atheists, will one day, when their illness is gone, relish God and revere Him.

I had to tell you so much about my truth for I desire that you should contemplate on this and derive joy therefrom, so that you may be inspired to observe the disciplines laid down and progress towards the goal of self-realization, the realization of the Sai that shines in your hearts.

- SATHYA SAI BABA

ILLNESS

One evening I was a guest speaker for a group of Realtors in St. Louis, I spoke on self-awareness, positive attitude, and motivation. When Robert and I left the meeting, we were surprised to find a major ice storm had moved into the St. Louis area. Everything was covered with ice, and the roads were treacherous. As Robert drove home, I encouraged him to wait until the salt trucks came, to make the roads less dangerous. But he was confident that if he drove slowly and carefully we would arrive safely. And we did!

At the time I had a strong intuition that this journey was significant and mentioned to Robert that there was an event in our future that would require us to travel over an uneasy path, steadily and slowly; but whatever it was, we would arrive safely. My words surprised even me. I was to look back on this event many times, clutching to the "hope," no, it was a "certainty," but surrounded by doubts, of arriving safely as I went through a long illness.

"The world itself is a great teacher, a constant guide and inspiration. That is the reason why man is surrounded and sustained by the world. Every bird, every animal, every tree, every mountain and star, even each tiny worm has a lesson for man if he has but the will and the thirst to learn. These make the world a veritable university for man; it is a Gurukul (school) where he is a pupil from birth to death."

When I heard that God was on earth in human form, I imagined that my problems would be removed. Some how they would all disappear. I was tired of the spiritual grind. So much inner work, and still the same problems would arise. I understood that evolution takes time but my time frame was not the same as the Lord's. I unconsciously set a time in my mind and I expected results. When my expectations were not met, I was in a state of despair.

About this time Sai sent us His 'calling card'. Hope reigned again in my heart, never did I suspect that I would have an additional hardship.

The date March 29, 1976 lives permanently in my memory. It was only one short month before, that Baba awakened me to His identity. I was still basking in the sunlight of knowing His Divine Form. I was in a state of gratitude knowing that God was here to remove my problems painlessly.

Swami's quotes like *"No, Pain; No Gain, or No Bumps; No Jumps"* were not a part of my vocabulary yet. Nor did I really understand how this spiritual game was played. I never dreamed that I had so much yet to learn. I became ill with a flu virus which developed complications. The second day of the virus I felt well; in fact, I had so much energy that I spent the day working. I was amazed at how quickly I had overcome the virus.

The following day it returned, only this time I felt dizzy. The symptoms grew more severe. I had motion sickness, nausea, dizziness, pressure in the inner ear and head, and extreme weakness. I felt as if I were on a rolling ship that sometimes was in a violent storm at sea. All I could do is lie flat with a cloth over my eyes because light bothered them.

I went to my doctor who sent me to a specialist in dizziness. He gave me some tests and his diagnosis was a viral infection had settled in the inner ear, disturbing my equilibrium. I was very sick. I was told that recovery would take about three months.

This sounded like an eternity. I was so sick and uncomfortable that it took all of my mental power to get through one day at a time. When the doctor told me three months, I felt as if it were a lifetime.

I have such great empathy for any person I see ill especially those who have a chronic or degenerating disease. I can remember my own inward struggle with illness and many are more severe than mine. I never enjoyed or felt comfortable being alone. If I was alone the radio, TV., or 'phone kept me company. When I was in pain or ill I craved even more for companionship. Everytime I was seriously ill circumstances would occur that prevented my husband from spending much time with me. This happened over and over again. I would ask, "Why is it when I need him the most, he is prevented from being with me?" It was not his fault. Life kept dealing me the same cards over and over again.

This illness was no exception. The same week that I became sick, Robert's company began a two-month strike. Since he was a manager, he worked twelve hours a day, seven days a week, to keep the plant running while the strike continued.

I was no help whatsoever. He not only had the extra hours at his work but also had extra work at home. It was a very stressful situation for both of us. I really was too sick to stay alone and after a few days I realized that I needed help. I called Mom. She would not come to our house because of Dad but I could come to her home.

I stayed with Mom for several weeks. I was not improving very much, so I went to get another doctor's opinion. They did more tests but could not find the cause. I soon became aware that whatever I had was being controlled by God and this experience was another big learning period for me. And all I could do was accept each day and do the best I could. I knew that I had NO CONTROL over my destiny.

As I said, being alone made me feel very uncomfortable. And this was my time to face it. I never felt so alone in all my life. Even when Robert and the children came home, I was too weak and sick to interact. I could not share or participate in their daily activities. They also had to add my workload to theirs. They were too busy to keep me company.

After being alone all day, I would crave to touch another person. It was my contact with the outside world. So many nights Robert would come home from work, and hold me in his arms so I could release my fears and tears.

"People suffer because they have all kinds of unreasonable desires and they pine to fulfill them and then they fail. They attach too much value to the objective world. It is only when attachment increases that you suffer pain and grief. If you look upon nature and all created objects with the insight derived from the Inner Vision, then attachment will slide away; though effort will remain, you will also see everything much clearer and with a glory suffused with Divinity and Splendor. Close the outer eyes and open those Inner Eyes and what a grand picture of essential unity you get! Attachment to nature has limits, but, the attachment to the Lord that you develop when the Inner Eye opens has no limit."

Since I had no where to run to, all I could do is lie flat in the dark, I was forced to face my fears and go inward and listen to God. He certainly got my attention. Since I loved activity normally God could never get me quiet for long enough to communicate. Now I had no choice, but to go inward.

Sai Baba taught me so much during this illness. He was teaching me to lean only on Him and to realize that we are never alone because God is our constant companion. The more my relationship with Sai Baba deepened, the less I felt alone. It was my body identity that I lost. I went back to the basic question. Who am I? I could no longer play the wife role, the mother role, the girlfriend role, the community worker role, etc., etc. Who am I? All the familiar roles were taken away, I became nothingness until I established a home and identity inside myself, that could not be shaken by the external enviornment.

Baba says, *"The Guru alone can open the inner eye and cleanse the inner instruments of intuition. He induces you to question yourself, Deham? Am I this body or is this body only a vehicle which I am using? He helps us discover the answer: Not I; I am not this Body. No, I am the Seer, the Witness, the Spectator. Then the investigation starts to delve into the reality of the I, who then am I? The answer reveals itself in the purified consciousness, I am He; I am a spark of that Glory I am Divine."*

In 1977, Dr. Hislop came to the Sathya Sai Baba Center in St. Louis and spoke on the spiritual practice of name and form. He told us that Baba says all we need to do to attain self-realization is visualize the form of God, any form that is familiar and pronounce His name, inwardly visualizing His form and repeating His name throughout the day. When we are working and cannot concentrate on name and form, we simply dedicate our work and our actions as worship to God. After we have completed our task, we continue to chant the name, out loud or silently inside, and visualize the form. So as I lay in stillness day after day, I practiced name and form.

29

"Have the Name of God on your tongue, in your breath, ever. That will evoke His Form as the Inner Core of everything, every thought, or turn of events. That will provide you with His Company, and contact with His unfailing Energy and Bliss. That is the good association that gives you maximum benefit. Talk with God who is in you, derive courage and consolation from Him. He is the Guru most interested in your progress. Do not seek the Guru outside you in hermitages or holy places. The God in you is Father, Mother, Preceptor, Friend."

I listened to Dr. Hislop's talk many times after that from a cassette. I was so happy to have something to listen to that lifted my spirit and reminded me of the real purpose of life. I could not participate in the outside world as I used to but now I was getting familiar with the inside space. Chanting His name gave my monkey mind something to occupy it's time. Illness and pain is a tremendous "mental trip."

I was suffering because of my attachment to my body but knowing this didn't help much because I could not change this thought pattern quickly, after years of association. In fact it just added one more thing to the list of spiritual attachments that was already too long to think about.

My moods changed frequently within a short period of time. For example in one hour, I could feel sorry for myself. I could feel courageous. I could gain insight and see the wisdom and goodness being extracted from this karmic action. I could become very depressed. Because of the intensity of pain or illness, the moods swung from high to low continually.

I became aware of the immense attraction the mind has for the body. Everytime I would focus on Sai Baba, the mind was snatched back to thinking about the body. I'd pull my attention again to focus on the Lord and like an elastic band it would snap right back to the body. Back and forth all day long, I was "pumping iron," only mental instead of physical. I was trying to develop a "Spiritual Muscle." After fighting to stay positive all day, I would be mentally worn out at night, emotionally low.

When Robert came home he cheered me up. I'd borrow his spiritual light when mine was gone. He was learning Sai Baba's teaching on selfless service. Doing service work in the home is more difficult because the ego gets less attention, less strokes. The ego is motivated many times because of ego rewards. In the home no-one knows what you do except your family and they have a tendency to take you for granted. Compliments are few and far between. You can learn how to serve others for a higher motive, selflessly.

Fear of the un-known kept on haunting my mind. After the first year there was very little improvement. The doctors were puzzled and could offer no diagnosis, I struggled with the thought of spending the rest of my life with this insane dizziness.

I was not in pain but extremely sick and uncomfortable. The see-saw movement created continual motion sickness, the kind that you get when you are sailing on a rough sea. It was so annoying. The dizziness and pressure in my head made thinking almost impossible and I would have to concentrate very much to perform any little chore or solve any problem. Sai was helping me to increase my power of concentration.

That was another whole aspect of this illness. The doctors were puzzled, but not Sai. I was aware that He was teaching me so many new behaviors. What was interesting was that this illness created symptoms that were a teaching media for most of my weaknesses. Baba had a teaching solution for every problem I had.

As I previously mentioned, He helped me to remove my fear of aloneness, to become acquainted with inner space, He increased my power of concentration, and taught me how to focus and depend more on Him for all my needs.

Next on the list were listening skills. I am a visual person. I learn primarily through my sight. If I see something written, I can remember. When it is only spoken, my retention is less.

My listening ability was poor compared to my sight or speech. There was an imbalance. I learned that listening takes greater concentration, and requires silence of body and mind. Since this illness created a fertile ground for developing my listening skill, I improved. I was not able to use my eyes for reading, or viewing TV. Therefore I was forced to listen, inwardly and outwardly. I spent the day listening to tapes and bhajans. I learned the Gayathri Mantra, a prayer, and had plenty of time for meditation.

The following quote of Sai Baba's is one I dearly love, on the principles of speech and sound.

"One of the first principles of straight living is the practice of silence. For the Voice of God can be heard in the region of your heart only when the tongue is stilled and the inner storm is stilled and the waves are calm. There will be no temptation for others to shout when you

talk to them in whispers. Set the level of the tone yourself as low as possible, as high as necessary, to reach the outermost boundary of the circle you are addressing. Conserve sound since it is the treasure of the element Akasa an emanation from God Himself. Reason can prevail only when arguments are advanced without the whipping up of sound. Silence is the speech of the spiritual seeker. Soft sweet speech is the expression of genuine Love. Hate screeches, fear squeals, conceit trumpets, but love sings lullabies; it soothes, it applies balm. Practice the vocabulary of love; unlearn the language of hate and contempt."

I liked to talk and I did so much. Sai was teaching me the value of silence and the art of listening. I was really weak and I quickly became aware of the vast amounts of energy needed to speak. I couldn't believe how much energy it took for one five minute conversation. If I talked on the telephone or with my family it would take me the entire day to recover. I was so weak. I was forced to discriminate daily between working on one household chore or a telephone call.

This illness created the perfect environment for learning, limited vision, speech and action. I was lying flat and quiet; looking inward and listening. I sincerely believe that without this prior experience, I certainly would not have been able to sit quietly and long enough to write a book.

Those experiences were spiritual exercises. In the beginning of the illness my eyes were sensitive to light; today, they are sensitive to darkness. Not the darkness that falls at night but the darkness of crime, injury to others, immodesty, violence and the exploitation of sex.

The Lord closed my eyes but opened my ears. He taught me to tune into His inner station. He saturated my ears with mantras, bhajans and discourses and made me deaf to gossip, profanity, and criticism. The tongue no longer constantly wags but enjoys lying still.

Now I love silence and enjoy being alone. I feel the closeness of His Presence with me. He has taught me to listen and only to balance this with speech and not loose the inner voice through conversations or chit-chat. I can sit in quiet solitude or become active, depending upon the circumstances. I am no longer 'crippled,' using only one leg or one aspect of myself, now I can walk more evenly with two legs with both the outer and inner aspects of myself in a more balanced way.

This illness was diagnosed as 'inner ear imbalance.' I guess His message to me was very clear "inner imbalance... here." He says, *"Man is sometimes very happy, sometimes he is afraid, and at other times he is courageous. These changes come about in quick succession and in a casual way. Let us examine the main reason for all these changes. The main reason for all these changes is the change that comes in our own mental attitude. These are manifestations of one's own qualities. There are Sathwic, Tamo, and Rajo gunas, or tendencies. If these three qualities are mixed in a balanced manner, there will be no drastic change in one's nature. Sunlight is composed of several different colors. When these colors are mixed in appropriate proportions, there will be no change and the sun will be shining in its natural color. On the other hand, if there is an imbalance in the manner in which these colors are mixed, then you will find that some special colors show themselves. In the same manner, if the Sathwic, Rajo, and Tamo gunas are mixed in balanced proportions, there will be no big change in what we see around us but if there is an imbalance and if one of the qualities has gained the upper hand, then you will find that there are drastic changes."*

So, Sai Baba taught me that I have three gunas tendencies that function within me. A guna is a human characteristic. The **Sathwic** Guna is the "white" quality—active, pure, good, calm, unruffled. The **Rajasic** Guna is the red quality—active, passionate, craves adventure, and activity. The **Thamasic** Guna is the "black" quality—dull, inactive, inert. It is the quiet aspect of the primal energy.

My Rajasic guna was working to its extreme. I thrived on activity. Something was always moving—hand, feet, or mouth, often all of them together! I could easily identify with outward activity. The inner activities of silence, stillness and aloneness were foreign agents to me. Baba started and is still teaching me to have a perfect balance or equilibrium between the three gunas. *"If the inner poise or inner equilibrium is undisturbed by external ups and downs, that is real success."*

My daily actions of work or play must be balanced with silence, rest and meditation. I must be prepared to handle each situation with the calmness and purity of the Sathwic guna. Baba taught me that not only must my actions be balanced but they should also be performed as a means of worshipping God.

"You have to busy yourselves with activity in order to

use time and skill to the best advantage. That is your duty, and duty is God. The dull and the inert will hesitate to be active, for fear of exhaustion or failure or loss. The emotional, passionate individuals will plunge headlong and crave for quick results and will be disappointed if they do not come in. The balanced persons will be active, because it is their duty; they will not be agitated by anything–failure or success. The godly will take up activity as a means of worshipping God and they leave the results to God. They know that they are but instruments in the hands of God."

Therefore, balanced activity free from praise or blame, expectations or agitations, offered to God as worship is my spiritual goal set by Sai Baba. If I wished to work for Sai Baba and help with His mission through His organization, then I must learn how to serve in the selfless manner He wishes. I must be taught how to surrender to God's Will; otherwise my ego will be working for my benefit instead of me making an offering to God.

I do not wish to mislead you into thinking I went through this period in a state of sainthood. Quite honestly, only because fifteen years have passed since then am I able to write objectively about this experience, stressing Sai's teachings instead of my misery. I also now recognize the profound changes in my behavior that have occurred as a direct result from this illness and Sai's teachings.

From March 1976 to September 1980, my health improved very slowly. Baba placed a live balance inside my head to measure imbalance. If I overindulged in any way, the scale inside rocked. I would have a relapse and spend a week or two in bed, waiting for the rocking to stop. It zapped my strength and left me weak. I became depressed. I was so tired of this chronic illness.

"Suffer loss and grief gladly; they help to toughen your personality. Seek the light always; be full of confidence and zest. Do not yield to despair; it can never produce results. It only worsens the problem, for it darkens the intellect and plunges you in doubt."

During this time, His words fell on deaf ears. I could no longer respond nor surrender. I wanted some relief! I lost hope and felt despair. Nothing I did seemed to work I cried out to Him for mercy.

My doctor admitted me to the hospital again for more tests. Several years had passed and perhaps something new would appear; but the tests revealed nothing. Oh God, I thought how will I ever be able to live with this forever?

Later that day, my physician suggested that I speak with a psychiatrist. Within five minutes, Dr. Soto diagnosed my illness as depression. He asked if anyone in my family had suffered from depression. I replied, "Yes, my mother has been on medication for 25 years." He told me that depression is hereditary and that I had a chemical imbalance in my brain. The last thing I wanted to hear was another IMBALANCE! He promised me relief in several weeks after taking an anti-depressant drug.

I had difficulty accepting his diagnosis. How could this doctor give me an answer in five minutes when others could not in four years? Could a cure possibly be so simple as popping a pill after all the health methods I tried? My thoughts flashed back. I grew wheat grass in my basement, extracted the juice and drank it daily. I fasted on water and watermelon juice for two weeks. I changed my diet to include health foods, no white sugar, starch, flour, and salt. I took vitamins. I worked on my mental attitude and visualized my cells being healed etc., etc.

Then I asked myself, how could a devotee on the spiritual path, be DEPRESSED? What a great blow to my "ego" and my image, of devotee? Is there nothing left unnoticed by this One with a thousand eyes and ears? He had chipped away, in these past years of my illness, the ego image of woman, wife, and mother. Meanwhile unnoticed by my newly trained "eagle eye" the image of devotee had slipped by.

I could hardly believe that taking a pill could make me feel so much better and bring relief from the turmoil in my head. I felt that Sai Baba had performed a miracle and I was so happy that my inner ear imbalance was finally still. How grateful I was and am to His mercy. I praised Him and thanked Him.

In the ensuing fifteen years, the symptoms still come back–not as severe but letting me know that something is unbalanced in my life. Sai Baba told me in an interview that He will heal me. I'm sure that will happen when His teaching aid has outlived its usefulness. Surrendering to the Lord's Will instead of 'mine' is a lesson that I shall not learn overnight. He tells us,

"For a tree to be born, to grow, and ultimately give you the fruit, there are three essential things. These are the wind, the rain, and the earth. More than these three, the seed is of even greater importance. If we do not have the seed, even if we have the other necessary ingredients like the earth, rain, and wind, we will not be able to see the

tree. In the same manner, it is in accordance with the sankalpa (desire) of the Lord that man is created in the world. Man comes into this world as if he comes from a seed. In the case of every man, the sankalpa that creates him is like a seed. So long as the sankalpa or desires are in man, it is not possible for him to escape being born. On the day when he becomes completely free from his sankalpa, or desire, that day will he be free from rebirth. In order that he may take this sacred path, free from desires, he has to surrender himself. There are certain obstacles for one to be able to surrender. Every one understands that in this world, it is not possible to enter the house of an affluent person or the house of a person who is in a position of importance with ease and without being questioned. At the entrance to the house, you will find a watchman or someone who will ask what business you have with the owner.

"If in the case of a person who has limited power and a worldly position, there are such restrictions regulating your entry into his house, are there not regulations restricting your entry into His mansion? If you want to enter the palace of moksha, or liberation, you will find that at the main entrance there are two guards. This entrance is the place where you offer yourself and may be called the gate of surrender. The two guards who are there are Srama and Dama. The meaning of this is that you must make an effort and you must have patience. These are the two guards at the door. However much you offer yourself in surrender, it is not possible for you to enter God's abode without Srama (effort) and Dama (patience)."

"There is no one to know who I am, until I created the world for my pleasure with one word. Immediately mountains rose up, immediately rivers started running, earth below, sky overhead, oceans, seas, lands and watersheds, sun, moon, desert sands sprang up from no where, to prove My existance. Then came all forms, human beings, beasts and birds, hearing, speaking, flying. The first place was granted to Mankind and My knowledge was placed in Man's mind."

BABA

INDIA

"**B**aba, here we come," I shouted within as the wheels of the plane lifted from the runway, knowing that I would experience God in human form before I returned to St. Louis. I gave a silent prayer for our safe journey and blanketed my family mentally with His love and grace, asking Him to care for them in our absence. Robert and I were ecstatic! It was hard to believe that we were finally leaving to see Baba. Since Sai identified Himself three years ago, we had silently dreamed of this day. I wondered how long our souls had waited for this opportunity?

I prayed that we would receive the maximum benefit from our visit. I so wished to learn from God how to become God. I wanted to fill my house with the same love that's in His house. I was eager to experience the daily life of an ashram and duplicate the spiritual atmosphere in my house. My goals were set before me. God only knows how much my home needed a spiritual atmosphere. I settled back into my seat, very conscious of my thoughts and feelings. I was savoring this moment as if it were the grandest feast my palate ever tasted, and I was full of contentment.

Sai Baba tells us that no individual can come to see Him unless they have been called by Him personally. We had three problems to solve before we could take this journey – children, my health, and money. Pat and Brian, devotees, offered to watch my children – indeed, a loving act of service. My health improved, and Robert was able to take out a loan from the credit union at work to pay for the trip.

A loan was a small investment for the Divine dividends we would receive from our journey to see Baba. I firmly believe that money is no excuse for continually postponing a trip to see Sai Baba. "Money is only a commodity of exchange," said Robert. "One day it's here; the next it's gone. It is as impermanent as our world. But the experience of the journey to see Sai Baba will last forever."

When we sincerely ask Him in our Heart if we can come to see Him, this wish He grants. Perhaps not at the moment we choose to go, but it happens when He wills us to go. Baba says, *"Many are called but few are chosen."* Rather many are called and few choose to answer. The desire and decision to go is ours. Once we say "Yes", He is responsible to fulfill this wish. It takes faith and courage to take this first step but it is our own choice to become one of the selected few. How many times in our lives do we let a good opportunity slip through our fingers? Don't add this one to your list.

The roar of the airplane engine insulates the mind from the exterior sounds and creates a fertile atmosphere for drifting inward, so I did. It was Holy week; Holy Thursday 1979, and hopefully we would have our first darshan on Easter Sunday. I was beginning to see a pattern emerge. For some reason Holy Week, usually in March or April, has been a marker for important spiritual events in our past. I remembered in 1969 during Holy Week that I had visions of the future and was told that the Lamb, Christ, in human form was on earth. Seven years later, March 1976, Sai identified himself as the Lamb, Ba–Ba, in human form living in India. Several weeks later, my illness reached its absolute worst during Holy Week, and I could vividly remember spending Holy Thursday, Good Friday, and Holy Saturday hanging onto the feet of Jesus and Baba because I was frightened and ill. Now, again Holy Week, and we were leaving to visit Sai Baba.

I hoped the symbolism of Christ's death represented for us the death of our ego, and His resurrection was a sign that Sai Baba would raise us to our divine heritage; Self-Realization the eventual goal of all souls, the final journey home.

Our first glimpse of India was the New Delhi airport. It was 3 a.m. and we were exhausted. I was looking for a place to rest after the ordeal of customs. There were no carpeted floors or upholstered seats. The look was austere. I noticed some of the Indian people were wrapped in a cover and were asleep on the floor. I wondered if I could do the same. I was very aware of not wanting to insult their customs by my Western behavior. I had been prepared and informed by the Sathya Sai Baba Council in America and the many devotees who had traveled before us. I finally decided to rest. I pushed our two big flat hard suitcases together to make one long bed, covered myself, and fell asleep for several hours until it was time for our Bangalore flight.

We had pre-arranged for a cab driver named Singh to meet us at Bangalore Airport. We had sent him a photograph, and were pleased when he met us. We relied entirely on his judgment and help in this strange new land. Singh told us Sai Baba was in Prasanthi Nilayam, so we decided to spend the night in Bangalore, to get a night's rest before we continued our last leg of the journey. We went directly to the Shilton Hotel, almost too tired to think or observe, but extremely happy to be this close to Baba.

Singh told us about three Italian ladies who wished to travel with us the next day. He gave us their room number and after resting, we introduced ourselves to them. I gave Singh a list so that he could shop for some supplies that we needed to take with us.

We visited the Italian ladies and offered to help in any way possible. One woman was completely blind and one was partially blind. The latter spoke a little English. The ladies had read about Baba in an Italian newspaper article and came directly over to see Him. We tried to answer their questions. Being new ourselves, we mostly relied on what we had been told instead of direct experience.

I asked them if they were aware of the dress code at Baba's ashram. They said they were not, so I informed them that Sai Baba wishes for all ladies to be fully covered. They could purchase a sari or a long skirt or dress, but the legs must be covered. If they chose the latter, then they would need a shawl or large scarf to cover their shoulders. The ladies decided to purchase a sari, and I promised to return and help with the 'wrapping'.

They called me after their purchase. I had only wrapped a sari twice before with the aid of an Indian friend, Kamal, in St. Louis. I was anything but proficient. I started with the blind girl first and said jokingly "This has got to be a perfect example of the blind leading the blind." We all laughed and giggled, as I wound the never ending yards of fabric around them.

The next morning they paraded out to the taxi, and I was utterly amazed at how great they looked. They seemed to be very pleased that they were appropriately dressed for Sai Baba's ashram. I admired their courage and determination.

It was summer in India, and because of the intense heat, Singh advised us to travel early. We left around 5 a.m. on Easter Sunday morning. Almost all the senses were flooded with foreign impressions, sights, sounds, smells, clothing, language, and food.

The streets were busy thoroughfares for cars, taxis, buses, rickshaws, people, bicycles, cows, dogs, motor scooters, etc. I could make out absolutely no sense or order concerning the traffic rules. It looked like a circus parade. The cars beeped their horns continuously, and the noise level was high. I stared in utter disbelief, feeling somewhat threatened but decided that since we had traveled 7500 miles safely in Baba's hands, the last few miles were not going to upset me. So I sat back, relaxed myself and decided to watch the show!

The scenery soon changed from the bustle of city life to a rural setting, a definite contrast. I felt as though I was tele-transported in a time machine and had arrived centuries ago. The cows and sheep meandered along the road, and women carried water on their heads. Oxen-drawn carts and plows were busy working on the land and small thatched huts clustered together to form the village communities. Occasionally we could see the temples and shrines along the roadside. The life-style told a story of hardship and simplicity. There were no telephone poles and wires, no billboards, and no electricity. The women cooked over an open fire, and that accounted for the smoke rising at each village in the early morning hours, as we traveled along. The day began early, to take advantage of the cool morning hours.

The land was basically flat with ranges of low hills, and occasional clusters of boulders as if burped-up from the depths of the earth, some quite massive in size. Occasionally, trees lined the road, providing shade for the many travelers. The road was rough and sometimes there was no pavement, only dirt and lots of dust.

The roads were built mostly with human machinery. There was no earth-moving equipment which was a common sight along the interstate highways in America. The local workers sat in a squatting position for endless hours beside the larger boulders, with a small hammer and chisel manually breaking the stones into small pieces of gravel. I could sense the endless hours of labor worked by many Indian people as the wheels of our vehicle rotated on the hard road.

The massive technological machinery and vast stretches of highway in the United States made a stark visual comparison between the lifestyles of these two different countries in my mind. I recalled this vision many times as I tried to accept and understand the people in this ancient land of India.

The Italian ladies asked how they could see Sai Baba. We told them Baba gave darshan twice a day, morning and evening. Darshan means seeing a holy person and receiving his blessing. Everyone gathered on the sands in front of the Mandir, or temple. There was a large enclosure where devotees sat. During darshan, Baba walks along the front row, took letters, blessed articles held out to Him, occasionally spoke and selected people for the treasured interview.

"How can we get an interview?" they asked. Baba alone makes that selection, as He gives darshan. No-one usually knows until He say's "GO!" We'd been told that it depends upon our past and present karma, the purity of our hearts, and Baba's Grace. If He comes near you during darshan, you can ask Him for an interview.

We arrived shortly after morning darshan, so we would have to wait till evening to see Baba. We checked in at the accommodation office and they assigned us a room in Prasanthi West. We had the traditional two-room apartment, sleeping room,with adjoining toilet area. It looked like an American basement, all cement but very small. There was a faucet next to the toilet used for bathing. It's called a "bucket bath." You fill the bucket with water and use a cup to pour the water over you. It is quite civilized and conserves water, essential in a hot dry climate.

How grateful I was that we took up camping six years ago. I'm certain that Baba was preparing us for this life. It would have been a bitter adjustment for me. Instead, we felt right at home, inflated our air mattresses, strung up a line to hang our clothes, set up our altar, unpacked our camping stove, and were grateful for indoor Western plumbing.

We met our neighbor, Catherine Bracey, a lovely soul from New Zealand. She answered our questions and shared her Baba story with us. Catherine was a permanent resident. As we spoke with her, I had this eerie feeling that Catherine was like a future me, and someday, I too, would live here.

The thought of living here permanently sent off a series of desires and interrupted my concentration while conversing with Catherine. "How could I ever live this simply? Could I ever stay alone without Robert? Camping like this is all-right, but everyday of your life? No ocean, no water, no mountains, and no grass." I pushed the feelings and thoughts out of my mind. It was too overwhelming for me to even look at since I had only just arrived. There were too many unknowns, and yet I could not deny my intuitive feelings.

There was an instant feeling of friendship, and we had three common loves – Sai Baba, Australia, and New Zealand. We fell in love with the warm and friendly Australians and the beauty of their country. The time for darshan finally arrived. Everyone was seated in the Mandir grounds, and I found a place near the rear wall next to some of Baba's high school girl students. I shook myself. Is this the video I'd watched so many times, or was I really here?

Almost immediately, the flash of orange appeared

on the veranda. Seeing His Divine form touched me deeply. The ache of longing for His presence stirred within me a rush of uncontrollable feelings. I tried to quieten the sobs that came forth from the pit of my stomach. I had never experienced a yearning or any desire that affected me so deeply as this.

"Yearning for God and constant contemplation on the Divine arises from innate urges derived from past lives."

As He walked closer, I could see His radiant smile. He is a picture of love and flowing grace. He is so small in stature, but His presence magnifies His greatness. His gestures are deliberate, His awareness superhuman. After observing Him during many darshans respond to so many people, so quickly, so accurately, it is super human. Such action alone is a proof of His Divinity.

Imagine if you had to locate just one person you knew in a crowd of thousands? And to add to its complication, you were to give ten messages, not written but spoken. Sai Baba can locate so many of us, give direct personal answers to our complex problems without us ever speaking a word. If He was human, the ego would have prevented His absolute attention given to others.

Just to give an example. There was a young American devotee whose co-workers would go to a bar after work to have a beer. He was invited to join them, but continually fought the desire. Knowing full well that Sai Baba does not approve of alcohol for spiritual aspirants, sometimes his desire won and he had a beer with the guys. Swami approached him in the darshan line, looked at him, and said, "Heineken today;

Heineken tomorrow!" This young man did not tell Sai Baba about his battle with the beer desire. Yet those few chosen words conveyed a profound message. Sai Baba speaks a few words, but communicates paragraphs. We speak paragraphs and communicate a few words.

I had my first conscious experience of Sai Baba's omnipresence several days after we arrived. As Baba came near me, he started chanting in fun, "Baba, Baba, Baba." It sounded like a mother mimicking her child calling "Mommy, Mommy, Mommy." I knew exactly what He was doing and why. He was imitating me. During my recent illness, I spent so many hours lying on the floor visualizing myself tugging on the bottom of His robe, just as a child, calling His name. . . Baba, Baba, Baba. In times of crisis, we can feel so inadequate and dependent, like a child.

"If you wail in agony, don't you hear me? My ears are there to listen. If you pray from the depths of your heart, don't you see my plight? My eyes are there shedding grace. I shall guard you as the lids guard the eye. I shall be beside you, behind you, before you, inside and outside, now and forever."

After darshan, Swami took a fortunate few inside for interviews. Bhajans then followed in the Mandir, singing praises to God, as Sai sat in His chair, keeping the rhythm with His hands. A bhajan is a song of praise to God.

"Not all realize the potency and efficacy of reciting the Lord's name. The first requisite is purity of thought, word, and deed. The name that is uttered by the tongue should be meditated upon by the mind. What is uttered and dwelt upon should be hailed by clapping the hands.

This three-fold concentration on the Divine name – unity of mind, speech, and action – purifies the heart and nourishes the feeling of devotion. The bhajans that are sung permeate the ether in the form of sound waves and fill the entire atmosphere, thereby purifying the whole environment. Breathing in this purified atmosphere purifies our hearts. Reciting the Lord's name is a process of give and take. Singing the Lord's name should become an exercise in mutual sharing of joy and holiness. It should be remembered that the sounds we produce reverberate in the atmosphere. They remain permanently in the ether as waves and outlast the individual uttering the sounds.

"Today the atmosphere is polluted by unholy and vicious sounds. This results in the growth of evil thoughts and feelings which lead to evil deeds. If the atmosphere is to be purified, it has to be filled with pure and sacred sounds, hence the need to cultivate purity in thought, word, and deed.

"Community bhajans should not be treated as a pastime. When thousands of persons join in singing bhajans, they should be fully absorbed in the devotional process and the ecstasy of that experience. The singing should be vibrant and soulful and not mechanical or drawling and uninspiring. It should combine feeling, melody, and rhythm. What delight can be experienced when all sing in chorus with the same feeling, in the same tune, and to the same timing! When there is such unity the Divine can be experienced."

After bhajans, Robert and I walked slowly to our room, sharing our first darshan experience with one another. Sai took the St. Louis devotees letters from Robert. We were so tired, but extremely happy. It had been a spiritual Easter, rejoicing in the presence of the Lord, Sai Baba. We ate a few fruits and nuts and settled into a peaceful sleep.

The day began early at Prasanthi. Omkar started at 5:00 a.m. in the Mandir. Omkar is chanting "om" twenty-one times, followed by Suprabhatham, the hymn to awaken the Lord. After the early morning greeting to God, the devotees lined up outside, men and women in separate lines for Nagarasankeerthan, the chanting of bhajans while walking in procession throughout the ashram.

That morning at darshan, Swami blessed me in many ways. I stared into His eyes and asked if we could have an interview. He patted my head and said, "Yes, I will give you an interview." He took the letters from my family and allowed me to have padnamaskar. I felt extremely uncomfortable trying to bend forward in a sari, sitting with my legs folded Indian-style, but I was determined to kiss His feet.

Padnamaskar is the sacred act of kissing the feet of the Lord. It is symbolic of surrendering our life to the will of God. *"It is not a question of surrendering or giving to some other one. One surrenders to oneself. Recognition that the Atma is oneself is surrender. Surrender really means the realization that all is God, that there is nobody who surrenders, that there is nothing to be surrendered."*

Then His hand moved in a circle and He materialized Vibhuthi and gave it to the lady next to me. I had actually seen a miracle and it happened before my own eyes!

Vibhuthi is a sacred ash, materialized by Sai Baba from the palm of His hand. Sai Baba uses this sacred ash to heal us physically and spiritually. It guards us and protects us. It is His spiritual prescription to take daily. It heals all diseases of body, mind and spirit. When it flows from His hand into ours, it is charged with His pure energy; and when we take it internally, it purifies and cures all ills.

"In the Bhrihad Upanishad, ash or Vibhuthi is equated with prosperity and one's spiritual splendor. As a talisman containing a divine secret, it also destroys danger and protects the one who wears this Sai ornament of purity. It is a silent messenger of detachment and renunciation, teaching the most elementary step of one's sadhana.

"Vibhuthi has also got an aspect of immortality, which makes it a fit offering for worshipping God. Flowers offered during worship will fade away, leaves will dry up, fruits will decay in course of time, and water will breed germs if left standing for any length of time. Only Vibhuthi remains unchanged as it is the final result of the five elements of creation. It is our desires which have to be reduced to ashes and Vibhuthi is symbolic of this renunciation and detachment."

All of our daily activities in the ashram provided a role model for us to follow after our visit. He teaches us how to fortify our life with spiritual practices, omkar, meditation, bhajans spiritual discourses, dwelling on the Lord and saying the Name. Then He gives us a "real life" experience, darshan, to practice "ego detachment". It didn't take long to realize that my concept of peace and serenity in Baba's ashram was a myth.

Darshan was a "group activity". Thousands of people from all over the world were massed together, all wanting the same thing – a front - row seat. It was a test bed that permits us to see our own level of detachment and self-discipline. Some of the games people played during this activity are pushing, shoving, running, squeezing in line, and going ahead of others. There was also ashram politics, special seating for special friends. Baba does not permit or approve of this conduct. These were not newly invented games, they have existed since the creation of the "ego"....the "I WANT" syndrome.

It is a sacred moment when we share together seeing God in human form. The unity of this experience, seeing God **with each other** needs to expand to seeing God **within each other**.

"The image, the form is not God, but all forms together, the totality of all forms can be taken as God. God is the reality behind the form. The world is there, but its reality is not seen. The reality is God. One may see the reality, that the truth behind every form is God. Once this perception arises, it is never lost. Although one sees the forms, he is always aware of the truth, the reality."

Darshan provides a classroom where we can experience and practice Sai's teachings in action. Some of the lessons are on discipline, discrimination, non-attachment, seeing God in the unpleasant, and self-inquiry. The following is a brief description of Swami's teachings on these subjects.

Discipline – *"For doing any kind of work in this world, there should be some order and discipline. Any work that you may do without discipline will not yield good results. In order to get this limitation in the worldly plane, some discipline is necessary. That which rules the world is the rule of law, discipline. This control of oneself is like tapas. A life in which there is not discipline* *and control will fail and fall one day or the other. If you put yourself on the wrong side of tapas which is pata, it means that you are going to fall. One must recognize the truth that there should be controls on and limits to human nature. The five elements that constitute the earth are also controlled by certain laws. Even the infinite ocean moves under certain laws and regulations. In the context of the whole world. Man's life is only a part and, therefore, man's life has to be regulated."*

Discrimination - *"There is another force in you through which God works and that is discrimination. That force must be used to put aside wrong action. The power of discrimination knows what is right and what is wrong. The wrong desire is God overshadowed by Maya, whereas discrimination is God less over-shadowing by Maya." "Use discretion and higher reasoning in order to discriminate the real from the unreal."*

Non-attachment *(Vairagya) "Vairagya means "renunciation" - not renouncing property and family ties, but renouncing the hold that the mind and the desires it breeds, has on you. Burn all traces of envy, pride, and greed. Fill your hearts with selfless Love. If you always repeat the idea of "mine, mine", how can you be useful to others? Sacrifice is the "salt" of life."*

Seeing God in the unpleasant Dr. Hislop, President of Sathya Sai Baba Council of America, asked Baba, "What is the art of looking whereby one may see the Lord even in unpleasant and disagreeable persons?" Baba answered, *"Even in persons of unpleasant nature, be aware that the Lord is in the heart even of that person. Have that aspect in mind and treat the person from that* *viewpoint to the best of your ability. In time, that person will respond, and his nature will change. One sees people as good or bad because he does not see the person in full, but only one-sided."*

Self-inquiry Hislop asked Baba, *"What is skillful self - inquiry?" Baba answered, "The devotee may not have any particular skill, but all can inquire of themselves if what they propose to do is right or wrong."*

Our negative character traits can be activated during darshan. A few of the old-time favorites are jealousy, envy, pride, and anger. Baba's image is one hundred percent pure, so as we sit in His Divine Presence, He reflects, like a mirror, a picture of ourself. It's easy to look into the mirror when the picture is good, but it can be unpleasant when the picture is bad. At first it may be a painful process, but as time evolves, we soon realize that once we look at our faults, they can be released and replaced. This simple act can purify our hearts and make us more receptive vessels to receive His selfless love and give this love to others.

Darshan has another purpose. Baba's magnetic love energy pulls on our hearts and is continually drawing us closer. After darshan, you can feel so close to Him. He manifests within us a desire to have His love and attention. While we sit in the darshan line, yearning, we physically experience what Sai Baba wants us to develop within ourselves, a closeness to God. When we taste the love and joy of being in His presence, it increases our desire for God-Consciousness, "Think God".

Baba says, *"There are three stages to knowing God.*

One is intellect, which is just imagination; one is drawing near; and third is union with God. Example: the river merges with the Ocean, but if one takes sweet water from the river and places it in a sealed plastic bag and places that sealed bag in the Ocean, there is no mixing of that water with the Ocean. Such a condition could be compared to one's state before coming here (Whitefield or Puttaparthi); but after coming here it is as though the sweet water were not held separate from the Ocean but were merged and mixed with the Ocean. This is the mixing stage, here."

On the surface it may appear that not much is happening while we spend countless hours waiting for Swami to come near. We can be fooled to think that this game of waiting is just to get a peek at His small orange form. But that's not true and I've explained to you that there is much more.

Let's compare it to an iceberg, floating in the cold icy waters of the Arctic Ocean. On the surface, you see only the tip, but underneath there is a massive structure that is very deep. The tip is only what meets the eye—the figure of Sai. But underneath, the inner significance is a massive structure of spiritual learning and exercise. As He makes His rounds on the darshan grounds, there is yet another gift that is unseen and extends far beyond the tip. His love bestows on us a supernatural gift.

"Always find a quiet corner after my darshan where you may enter the stillness and receive the completion of my blessings. __My energy goes from Me as I pass by.__ If

you proceed to talk with others immediately, the previous energy is dissipated and returns to me unused. Rest assured that whatever my eyes see becomes vitalized and transmuted. You are being changed day by day. Never underestimate what is being accomplished by this act of darshan! My walking among you is a gift, yearned for by the God's of highest Heaven and here you are daily receiving this Grace.

"Be grateful; these Blessings you receive will express themselves in their perfect time. But also remember that to whom much is given, from him much is demanded!"

During the next four days, Swami showered His love and attention on Robert and I. He spoke with us, signed our pictures, blessed our articles, patted our heads, and allowed us to take padnamaskar. How nice it was to bask in the warmth of His sun! One morning, Robert returned from Omkar with a beautiful garland for our altar. I suggested since it was our first garland, let's offer it to Sai as a gift of thanks for this lovely trip.

He took the garland to darshan, and Swami accepted it. We were extremely pleased. It was a short darshan because Baba suddenly left for Bangalore, much to our surprise. Everyone at the ashram was hustling to get a taxi and packing for their trip to join Sai Baba. We decided to spend this last day in Prashanti and travel to Bangalore in the morning.

All the spiritual activities at the ashram continued except for darshan. That evening we went to bhajans in the Mandir, and around the neck of Shirdi Sai was placed what appeared to be the garland that we had given to

Sai. I've never asked Swami if it was ours, but Robert and I both had the same experience upon seeing it on the altar. We cried and questioned, why Shirdi Sai?

Recently, after we returned from our seventh trip, we had a reading from the Book of Brighu, which is described in chapter 18. In the reading, we were told that Robert and I were both married and devotees of Shirdi Sai in our previous life. We wondered if that was why Swami put the garland around Shirdi Sai's neck?

OOTY

Baba has a college for men in Whitefield, just outside Bangalore. The ashram there is sometimes referred to as his Brindavan Residence. Baba had given no darshan since we arrived on Friday morning, and this was Sunday. We arrived late for early-morning Omkar because our driver overslept. We had just missed Baba's balcony darshan. There was a rumor that Baba was leaving for Ooty, and everyone rushed to the gate to receive his car darshan. We were not familiar with Ooty, but since we only had three weeks' vacation, we wanted to follow Sai. I stood in line pleading with Baba in my heart to let us join Him in Ooty. As the car passed, Baba had His back to me. It appeared that He was ignoring me, but I knew better.

We asked our cab driver if we could join Baba, and he replied, only if we had Sai's permission. We left

Brindavan feeling sad and empty, but resigned to Sai's will, and prepared to wait for His return. As we entered our room at the Shilton, a woman devotee, Nancy, who occupied a room across from ours, called out to ask us about morning darshan. Why had we returned so early? I told her that Baba had left for Ooty. She beckoned us to come to her room. She said, "Are you sure they said Ooty?" She told us to have a seat, and she would call some of the other devotees from the States. There seemed to be a lot of excitement about Ooty.

Nancy talked with our cab driver and found out that he had an injured knee and didn't wish to go to Ooty. She felt certain that we were to go, especially since we only had one week before we returned to the U.S. Nancy made all traveling arrangements for us. We were to share a taxi with Janice and Jan Nigro, a very sweet couple. Baba had inadvertently taken care of everything. We were so new and inexperienced, it was extremely comforting to have the help of other devotees.

The Nigros were married by Swami one year before. They told us their story. Baba materialized their wedding rings and gave Janice a beautiful silk sari. This week they were celebrating their first Anniversary. How uncanny that these two people had experienced in reality our dream to have Swami remarry us and materialize wedding rings. I had never thought of a silk sari or a one-year anniversary trip to Ooty, but these ideas found fertile ground to grow a new desire in my mind, especially after I saw Ooty.

OOTY

The scenery was spectacular. It was a seven-hour taxi trip, driving across the plains, through forests, jungle, and mountains. The mountain views were breathtaking, and the road was very narrow. The Nigros and Bruces were very compatible, and the journey was a pleasant one. It was so cool in the mountains–a sweet relief from the summer heat in Prasanthi. All the foliage was a lush green and flowers bloomed everywhere. No wonder there was so much excitement about Swami traveling to Ooty.

Ootacamund is a picturesque small town that winds itself around the mountain slopes. It was once a British Hill Station and the home of the Maharajah's Summer Place. The Palace was converted into a hotel that retained the nostalgia and grandeur of its time. The town is noted for its tea-growing industry and tourism. The cool climate welcomes the wealthy as a vacation retreat from the summer heat.

Sai Baba's school, in Ooty is for the primary grade students. It is located on the hillside overlooking the manicured tea gardens, so prominent in this town. I felt as if I was in the Garden of Paradise. Flowers, large pine trees and hedges aligned the driveway leading to the school, ending in a circle with a fountain and garden at its center.

The students were in uniform, wearing brown short pants or skirts, long knee socks, and orange sweaters the color of Baba's robe. The first thing I noticed were their smiling, radiant faces. This is a boarding school and the children are separated from their parents, brothers and sisters, but their faces show such happiness.

Baba   tells us that once we become a student or devotee of His, and begin to live a pure spiritual life, He becomes the parent.   *"Consider the meaning of the name, Sai Baba. Sa   means 'Divine'; ai or ayi means 'mother,' and Baba means 'father.' The name indicates the Divine Mother and Father. Your physical parents exhibit love with a dose of selfishness; but this Sai "Mother and Father" showers affection or reprimands, only for leading you toward victory in the struggle for self-realization."*

It was morning darshan, and there were only about one hundred people gathered in front of the school. Baba was scolding two ladies next to me. He said they were bad! I kept smiling at Him, and occasionally he would look. The mother sweetness of God was still very much present, even when He reprimands us.

When   He came to me, I again asked, "When is our interview, Baba?" *"Yes, yes,"* He replied, and I kissed His feet. When His eyes met mine, my heart seemed to melt into surrender.

Robert and I had written a note asking if we could stay for one additional week. Swami stood and read Robert's note, then asked, *"When are you leaving?"*

"This Thursday."

"Thursday," said Baba, *"two more days."*

"Yes", replied Robert.

Baba said, *"I'll see you tomorrow."*

We were really excited!

I put on my best sari, prepared my heart to be open

and went over my list of questions for Baba. Janice helped us gain confidence for our interview with Sai. She said many times people got an interview with Baba and became speechless. She stressed the importance of being prepared with a list of questions. The opportunity of sitting before the Lord is rare, so make good use of the time.

Selection of questions important enough to ask Swami is a spiritual exercise in itself. It teaches us discrimination of thought, word and deed. It was April 24, 1979, morning darshan. The air was pure and cool, the sky blue and it was our day for an interview. I knew in my heart that it was our time. When Baba called Robert to "go", for an interview, my heart began pounding. All of a sudden my legs became weak, and I had difficulty rising. I stepped on my sari, and the papers in my lap scattered on the ground. I must be having an anxiety attack! I pleaded to Sai, please give me time to compose myself...I don't want to miss a beat of this interview.

I was the last to enter, following Baba. There were nine people–two Indian men and one woman, two Indian sisters, and the two Italian ladies that we shared our cab with when we first arrived. We stood in the hall, and in the adjoining room were Baba's school children. They stood in rows, facing Baba and sang two bhajans, one in English and one in Telugu. They used their hands for gestures and appeared to be very disciplined. Baba's sweetness poured on the children.

After hugging some of the young boy students, Sai

took us into the interview room, and we had chairs to sit on. Baba had all of us sit down while He talked with the two Indian men and women. They were consulting Sai about surgery. He was giving me time to calm myself down. I don't ever remember my heart pounding so hard. After completing their talk with Baba, the three people left and six of us remained for an hour interview.

Baba asked Robert, *"Where are you from?"*

"St. Louis," Baba.

"It's very far," said Baba.

Swami directed Robert to move to a better seat, immediately across from Him. *"What are you doing for sadhana?"* asked Swami.

Robert stuttered, "Reading."

"No," said Baba, *"experience, experience, experience".*

"How do you feel?" He asked Robert.

"I'm a little scared," he replied.

"How do you feel, physically?" said Baba.

Robert answered, "I have a few aches, but its normal."

Swami was speaking to us like a concerned parent. He was helping us to relate to Him in a human way. We were feeling more at ease. This was a rare occasion. How many times does one sit down with God, in His parlor, for a friendly chat? Suddenly the simplicity of the conversation was changed to a spiritual topic, and the Divine nature of Sai Baba took the lead.

He looked into our eyes, using His hands to gesture, and said, *"Who am I? Am I this arm, this limb, this body, this mind? No, I am none of these things. Who am I? I am God,* He answered. He turned to Robert, pointing with his finger, and asked, *"Who are you? You are God, and I am God. You and I make we, and we are God. The only difference between us is that I know it and you do not. God is love. Love is so important. God is omnipresent, everywhere. Love all of God's creation.*

"When you are born, you are called a child, then a mother or father, then a grandfather or grandmother. You are called by many different names, but you are the same person. The same is true of God. God is one, but called by many different names. There is only one God.

"The Trinity in the Bible is the same as the Hindu Trinity, adwaita (principal that God and Soul are the same.) First, you are messengers of God. Then you are sons of God; there is God and you. Next, you become the Father, and you and God are one.

"Some people think, some people speak, and some act. Their thoughts are not the same as their words, and their words are different from their actions. The thoughts, words, and acts must be one. The desires create the mind, no desire–no mind...only God. The cross represents crossing out the ego, the I. Cut off the head of the ego.

"Before marriage you have two legs, after marriage four legs–male child, six legs, girl child, eight legs. The load is very heavy with duty. Duty is first–love without attachment. My husband, my son, my sister. Who is this MY? Lighten your attachments, it is easier to travel with

less luggage, but duty is first."

Baba asked Robert, *"Who are you? You are man, a part of mankind. Mankind is very evil. Man without morals has no character."*

Swami asked Robert, *"Where is your wife?"* Robert pointed. Baba looked at me and laughed. (Since I was the only American lady, the answer was obvious and everyone laughed.)

Baba said, *"Yes, I know. How does your wife feel?"*

Bob said, "She is sick."

Baba replied, *"I know, her health is not good."*

I asked, "Baba will you please help me?"

Swami answered, *"I will make you some Vibhuthi and put it on your head."*

"What work do you do?" asked Baba.

"I'm an engineer", said Bob.

"What does your wife do?"

"She's a homemaker."

"Well", Baba replied, *"sometimes she gets angry.* He shook His finger at me with a twinkle in His eye. *The anger is quick, but she is over it right away."* Baba said, *"The emotions."*

Baba took the two Italian ladies behind a screen that made a temporary partition. We found out later that the blind lady wanted to touch Swami's hair, and He let her feel it. He also talked briefly with the two Indian ladies and materialized Vibhuthi.

Robert asked for a private interview and Baba said we would have one in Bangalore.

"Will you marry us?," asked Robert.

"Yes, in Bangalore."

Sometime in the middle of our interview, Robert asked Baba if we can stay for another week? I pleaded, "Please, can we stay, Swami?" Baba laughed and there was a long pause.

He then said, *"Baba is thinking."*

I para-phrased Baba, "Did you say Baba is thinking about us staying?"

"Yes, Baba is thinking."

At the close of our interview, Baba walked over to Robert and said, *"You stay, and cable home,"* in a commanding tone.

Swami returned from behind the screen with two large bags filled with Vibhuthi packets. The ladies took the end of their saris folded them over and Baba put the Vibhuthi inside the sari. I did the same and Swami said, *"No, in your hands,"* and filled them. When He finished distributing the Vibhuthi, He came to me.

"Baba, what is the cause and how can I correct my dizziness?"

He very sweetly took my hand and said *"Private interview in Bangalore."* I kissed His hand. He said, *"Be happy! Time is most important. Don't waste a moment.*

Time is very precious to you. Life is a bubble, it floats up and down. Joy is a brief interlude between two sorrows. Without sorrow, there will never be any joy." The interview ended.

His love and joy bubbled up within us. We left the interview room filled to capacity. The light of His love energy shone in our eyes. Instead of walking, I felt as if I were floating.

We went to lunch and shared with Janice and Jan our interview. How grateful we were to have someone to share this experience with. After lunch we went to our room, sat down, and recalled the interview and carefully wrote His words in our diary. It takes time to digest the spiritual food that Baba gives us.

Before our trip, I was asked by a devotee in Chicago if I would participate in a panel discussion on Self-Realization for the Central Regional Conference. I consented. After I hung up the phone, on the inner level I told Swami, "I am not qualified to speak on Self-Realization, only you are. Please give us a discourse on Self-Realization so I can bring your words to the devotees from the Central Region." It took me two days before I became aware that the topic of His discourse to us in our interview was Self-Realization!

The interview was woven with threads of meaning for us. The point of His needle pricked our ego, but His stitches of love mended the heart quickly.

He answered some of my questions even though they were never asked. Baba controlled most of the conversation. He spoke of my health, letting me know of His concern and the location of my problem–my head. He also knew Robert's source of pain–his mind.

Robert and I were deeply involved and struggling with the duty and responsibility of raising our children. Swami recognized this burden with His story of adding legs in marriage. When He asked "who is" my wife? my child? who is this my? He was telling us to detach from our children's problems. Whose child was having the drug problem? Was this child really ours or His?

When Sai asked, Robert, "Where is your wife?" It was a question that had a double meaning. When Robert pointed to me, Swami said, "I know, I know." He was letting Robert know that I was his wife, because Robert often questioned whether I am the correct wife for him in this life. He felt that perhaps someone else would suit his personality better and cause him less conflict. Baba was assuring him that I am the correct wife for him.

He uncovered my temper. Swami knew that I have a short fuse. It must come with the red hair! My emotions move so fast, the words are out before I know what I've said, and how do you take it back? Once we have hurt someone with our speech, it's too late, the damage is permanent. There is no eraser to wipe out spoken words, only written ones.

"The tongue is given the job of speech. It is a tool that you can use in order to give vent to your thought, your

ideas, your feelings, your desires, your prayers, your joy, your sorrows. If you are angry, you use it to speak out harsh words very loudly. If you are pleased, you use it to speak soft words, in a low pleasant voice. I want you to use your tongue only for your good and the good of others. If you speak harshly to another, he too talks loud and harsh; angry words cause more angry words. But if you use soft and sweet words when another is angry towards you, he will calm down, he will be sorry that he used his tongue in that way. Do not shout, do not talk longer than necessary, do not talk when there is no need to talk; when you speak to someone or some group of friends, raise your voice to the pitch that is just right for the listener or listeners and not more. Why should you waste your energy to talk louder and longer than necessary?"

When Swami came over to speak with me privately, He told me to be happy. I was not happy. He also knew my desire was to advance spiritually, so He reinforced the necessity of using my time efficiently. He also was telling me that joy and sorrow are a natural condition of life. I was filled with sorrow because of our problems. He was letting me know that He understood.

Evening darshan was magnificent. If you came early, and were prepared to wait, there was always a front row seat in Ooty. The numbers of people increased each day, but compared to Prasanthi this was certainly a great opportunity to be close to Baba daily. I felt as if the Lord was romancing us in Ooty.

Suddenly the devotees were standing up and rushing

toward the door of Baba's school. I was told that Baba had invited us in for evening bhajans with the school children. I walked because I knew that running was not fulfilling Swami's wish, and I was one of the last to enter.

By a stroke of Sai's grace, a strange thing happened. I started to sit in the very rear, but it was so crowded. A lady volunteer motioned for me to come forward. I did. Then another lady volunteer motioned for me to come still closer, my final destination, was next to Baba.

I was seated by the side of Swami and could see the faces of the little students. I observed the interaction of love between Baba and the children. What I experienced is best summed up by Baba's words on love. *"The more it is shared, the deeper it becomes, the sweeter its taste, and the vaster the joy."*

The children's love for Sai was a perfect example of "one-pointedness." Their little eyes were never distracted from Baba. I was amazed. How could children this young sit quietly for thirty minutes without turning their heads? Again this question is answered by His Words. *"By Means of love, one can approach God and stay in His Presence, for God Is love and when one lives in Love, he is living in God."*

The next day we placed a telephone call home. Pat said that she had had a Baba dream and knew that we were staying longer. She also knew that we had an interview. (I wondered had Baba meant that He would send the message to her?) Our news was old news. She was certainly on target. She didn't mention to us at the time, but she had become ill with a very bad 'flu and had to take care of my family under extremely difficult circumstances. Perhaps that was why Swami hesitated in giving us an answer.

I was so impressed with the behavior of the students. I wanted to talk with the teachers and learn about Baba's school program. I was told that I would need Baba's permission before the teachers could share their program with me. So I wrote a note to Baba.

During darshan, Baba did not come near the section where I was sitting. But after He finished the men's darshan, He looked over to where I was. He walked over and said, *"RITA"*, rolling his R's, He took my note and read it, then He made a sound like hummmmmm. I guessed He was thinking again! I must admit His action left me speechless.

I wondered if it has any meaning when the Lord pronounces our name? The sound of Baba calling my name vibrated inside me, feeling similar to the OM vibration only much stronger. I wondered if He would give me an answer to my note?

Also during darshan, Swami looked at Janice's wedding ring, and said, Wedding one year ago, I'll see you tomorrow."

The next morning Janice wore her wedding sari, and Baba gave them a wonderful anniversary gift–an interview. Now it was their turn to share with us over lunch. We could feel Swami's love through them. It was like taking a piece of sweet chocolate from someone else's box.

We were free to communicate and share Baba's attention with each other because we were both receiving His grace. When there is equal attention given by God to others, jealousy is less likely to occur. Yet sometimes in our excitement, we share our good fortune with people who are wanting the same, and our actions can open the door of jealousy for others and pride for ourselves.

Jealousy and pride are two enemies that Swami is trying to prevent within us, so it is a mistake to use His stories to create what He is trying to destroy. *"Spiritual pride is the most poisonous of all varieties of pride; it blinds and leads the person suffering from it into ruin. Beware of pride; be always aware that you are but instruments in my divine mission."*

The next morning, Robert was blessed by Sai. He gave Swami a thank-you note and as he bent down to kiss His feet, Sai materialized Vibhuthi for Robert.

What a joy! Robert said that the taste, color, and texture was different to that which comes in the packets. I sat across from Robert and I could see Swami's loving gestures to Robert. Sai is always so gentle with our fragile hearts.

The next day, April 27, Baba left for Bangalore before darshan. The four days of bliss had come abruptly to an end. It felt like we had escaped to heaven for a brief interlude, but now it was time to face the reality of life. As we traveled down the mountain - side, the pain of leaving reminded me of the child who doesn't want to leave his first birthday party.

Robert was sick and burning with a high fever. He was quite uncomfortable traveling for the seven-hour journey. After we arrived at the Shilton Hotel, Robert took a shower and went to bed.

I was going next door to the Ananda Bhavan to have dinner. Asha, the daughter of the owner, Dr. Gupta, was going to fix some dinner for me and something special for Robert. Bob felt so sick that he refused to go to dinner.

I noticed that he had taken off his Baba ring before he showered and it was sitting on the dresser. It was a little metal ring that he purchased and Baba blessed. I said, "Robert, here's your ring." He put it on, and within two minutes he felt well enough to walk next door and have a light dinner. He felt fine thereafter. We wondered if the Vibhuthi that Swami materialized for him was performing some kind of cleansing.

The following day Swami took my note asking if I could talk with Mrs. Padmanaban, who is convenor of the Bal Vikas Program for the state. After darshan I received a written invitation to a cultural program being performed by the Bal Vikas children, on May 2.   Dr. R. S. Padmanaban, presiding,–the husband of the woman I wished to meet. I hurriedly took out my pocket calendar to check our date of departure. It was on the day before we were to   leave.   I had heard about the lovely performances of the Bal Vikas children and I was really delighted to receive the invitation.

Shortly, after this, I was introduced to Mrs. Kamal Padmanaban by Ellen, a devotee, and she invited us to come to her home on the morning of the cultural program. She was most helpful. She answered my questions about Bal Vikas, supplied me with materials, and shared with us some of her experiences.

Day by day, we waited for the promised second interview. Swami said He would marry us and answer my questions concerning my health in Bangalore. The anxiety built up as the days dwindled to the last one. As He passed, I inquired about our interview. He said, "Yes, yes, I will see you," and patted my head. Only the Lord knows the time of our next interview. If we didn't swallow the hook of desire and get tangled in our ego, we would have been free to swim away unconcerned. However, we swallowed the hook, line and sinker! Our disappointment soon faded into gratefulness, because He had given us so much of His time and help.

After darshan, we visited Baba's tailor, Mr. Rao. He had done some sewing for me. Mr. Rao had just received some calendars from Baba that He signed, and he gave us one. It was like a farewell gift from Baba and a keepsake of our trip.

Our months absence was apparent when we arrived home. Our work was waiting. What an overwhelming sight! The added features were a broken washing machine and a car that wouldn't run. The teen - agers unloaded their weeks' grievances with each other, and I wondered if India was a dream. "I know," Baba had said "head in the forest; hands in society."

Shortly after I arrived home, I stumbled across a discourse that Swami had given on March 2, 1970. He outlined the rules for managing a school. He answered the question (on school rules) I asked in Ooty and can be found in the chapter on Parents.

"God, first;
the world next;
myself last!"

BABA

November 23, 1990 Fiftieth Golden Jubilee of His Mission

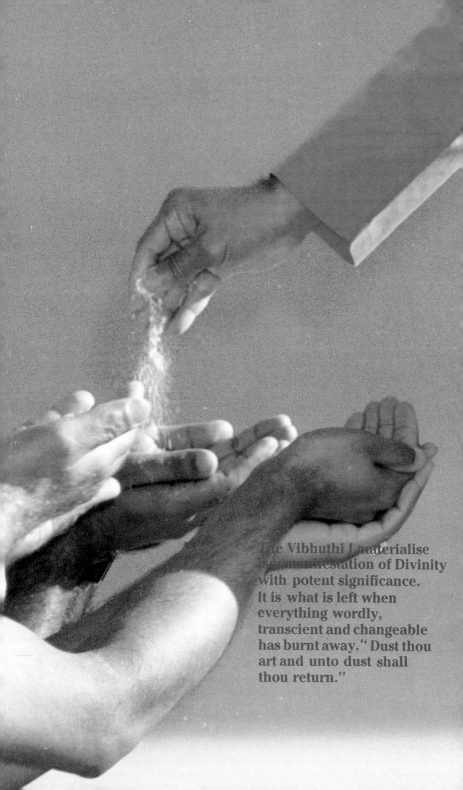

The Vibhuthi I materialise is a manifestation of Divinity with potent significance. It is what is left when everything wordly, transcient and changeable has burnt away." Dust thou art and unto dust shall thou return."

WHY I INCARNATE

DIVINE DISCOURSE

*F*or the protection of the virtuous, for the destruction
of evil-doers, and for establishing righteousness on a firm
footing, I incarnate from age to age. Whenever ashanti,
or disharmony, overwhelms the world, the Lord will
incarnate in human form to establish the modes of earning
prashanti, or peace, and to re-educate the human
community in the paths of peace.

At the present time, strife and discord have robbed
peace and unity from her family, the school, the
community, the society, villages, the cities, and the state.
The arrival of the Lord is also anxiously awaited by
saints and sages. Sadhus prayed, and I have come. My
main tasks are fostering of the Vedas and fostering of
the devotees. Your virtue, your self-control, your

detachment, your faith, your steadfastness–these are the signs by which people read of my glory.

You can lay claim to be My devotee only when you have placed yourself in My hands fully and completely with no trace of ego. The Avantar behaves in a human way so that mankind can feel kinship, but rises into his superhuman heights so that mankind can aspire to reach the heights and through that aspiration can actually reach Him.

Realizing the Lord within you as the motivator is the task for which He comes in human form. Avatars like Rama and Krishna had to kill one or more individuals who could be identified as enemies of the dharmic way of life and thus restore the practice of virtue. But now there is no one fully good. And so who deserves the protection of God? All are tainted by wickedness, and so who will survive, if the Avatar decides to uproot? Therefore, I have come to correct the 'buddhi' the intelligence by various means. I have to counsel, help, command, condemn, and stand by as a friend and well-wisher to all, so that they may give up evil propensities and, recognizing the straight path, tread it and reach the goal. I have to reveal to the people the worth of the Vedas, the Shastras, and other spiritual texts which lay down the norms. If you accept Me and say "Yes," I, too, respond and say "Yes." If you deny and say "No," I also echo "No." Come, examine, experience, have faith. That is the method of utilizing Me.

I do not mention about Sai Baba in any of My discourses. Though I bear the name as Avatar of Sai Baba, I do *not appreciate in the least the distinction between the various appearances, of God - Sai, Rama, Krishna, etc. I do not proclaim that this is more important or that the other is less important. Continue your worship of your chosen God along the lines already familiar to you. Then you will find that you are coming nearer and nearer to Me, for all names are Mine and all forms are Mine. There is no need to change your chosen God and adopt a new one when you have seen Me and heard Me.*

Every step in the career of the Avatar is predetermined. Rama came to feed the roots of Sathya, or truth, and Dharma, or righteousness. Krishna came to foster Shanti–peace–and Prema, love. Now all these four are in danger of being dried up. That is why the present Avatar has come. The Dharma that has fled to forests has to be led back into the villages and towns. The anti-dharma that is ruining the villages and towns has to be driven into the jungle.

I have come to give you the key of the treasure of Ananda, or bliss, to tell you how to tap that spring, for you have forgotten the way to blessedness. If you waste this chance of saving yourselves, it is just your fate. You have come to get from Me tinsels and trash, the petty little cures and promotions, worldly joy and comforts. Very few of you, desire to get from Me the thing I have come to give you, namely, liberation itself. Even among these few those who stick to the path of Sadhana, or spiritual practice, and succeed, are a handful.

Your worldly intelligence cannot fathom the ways of God. He cannot be recognized by mere cleverness or intelligence.

You may benefit from God, but you cannot explain Him. Your explanations are merely guesses, attempts to cloak your ignorance in pompous expressions. Bring something into your daily practice as evidence of your having known that secret of the higher life from Me. Show that you have greater brotherliness; speak with more sweetness and self-control. Bear defeat as well as victory with calm resignation.

I am always aware of the future, the past as well as the present of every one of you. So, I am not so moved by mercy. Since I know the past, the background, the reaction is different. It is your consequence of evil deliberately done in the previous birth, and so I allow your suffering to continue, often modified by some little compensation. I do not cause either joy or grief; you are the designer of both these chains that bind you. I am Anandaswarupa. Come, take Ananda from Me; dwell on that Ananda, or bliss, and be full of Shanti or peace.

My acts are the foundations on which I am building my work — the task for which I have come. All the miraculous acts which you observe are to be interpreted so. The foundation for a dam requires righteous materials; without these it will not last and hold back the waters. When the Lord is incarnated, He has to be used in various ways by man for his uplift.

The Lord has no intention to publicize Himself. I do not need publicity, nor does any other Avatar of the Lord. What are you daring to publicize Me? You speak one thing about Me today and another tomorrow. Your faith has not become unshakable. You praise Me when things go well and blame Me when things go wrong. When you start publicity, you descend to the level of all those who compete in collecting plenty by decrying others and extolling themselves. Where money is calculated, garnered, or exhibited to demonstrate one's achievements, I will not be present. I come only where sincerity and faith and surrender are valued; only inferior minds will revel in publicity and self-aggrandizement. These have no relevance in the case of Avatars; they need no advertisement.

The establishment of dharma–righteousness that is My aim. The teachings of dharma, the spread of dharma that is My object. These miracles, as you call them, are just a few means towards that end. Some of you remark that Ramakrishna Paramahansa has said that the siddhis, yogic powers, are obstructions in the path of the sadhaka. Yes, siddhis may lead the sadhaka, or the spiritual aspirant, astray. Without being involved in them he has to keep straight on or his ego will bring him down to the evil, the temptation of demonstrating his yogic powers. This is a correct advice which every aspirant should heed. But the mistake lies in equating Me with the sadhaka like the one whom Ramakrishna wanted to help, guide, and warn. These siddhis, or yogic powers, are just in the nature of the Avatar. The creation of peace with intent to protect and give joy is spontaneous and lasting. Creation, preservation, and dissolution can be accomplished only by the Almighty. No one else can. Cynics carp without knowledge.

They who learn the Shastras, or Scriptures, or they

who cultivate direct experience can understand Me. Your innate laziness prevents you from the spiritual exercises necessary to discover the nature of God. This laziness should go. It has to be driven out of man's nature in whatever shape it appears. That is My mission. My task is not merely to cure and console and remove individual misery; but it is something far more important. The removal of misery and distress is incidental to My mission. My main task is the re-establishment of Vedas and Shastras and revealing the knowledge about them to all people. This task will succeed. It will not be limited. It will not be slowed down. When the Lord decides and wills, His Divine will cannot be hindered.

You must have heard people say that Mine is all magic, but the manifestation of Divine power must not be interpreted in terms of magic. Magicians play their tricks for earning their maintenance, worldly fame, and wealth. They are based on falsehood and thrive on deceit. But this Body can never stoop to such a low level. This Body has come through the Lord's resolve to come. That resolve is intended to uphold Sathya, or truth. Divine resolve is always true resolve. Remember, there is nothing that Divine power cannot accomplish. It can transmute earth into sky and sky into earth. To doubt this is to prove that you are too weak to grasp great things and the grandeur of the universe.

I have come to instruct all in the essence of the Vedas, to shower on all this precious gift, to protect Sanatana Dharma–the ancient wisdom–and preserve it. My mission is to spread happiness, and so I am always ready to come

84

among you, not once, but twice or thrice, as often as you want Me.

Many of you probably think that since people from all parts of India, even from foreign countries, come to Puttaparathi, they must be pouring their contributions into the coffers of the Nilayam. But let Me declare the truth. I do not take anything from anyone except their love and devotion. This has been My consistent practice for the last many years. People who come here are giving Me just the wealth of faith, devotion and love. That is all.

Many of you come to Me with problems of help and mental worry of some sort or the other. They are mere baits by which you have been brought here, but the main purpose is that you may have the grace and strengthen your faith in the Divine. Problems and worries are really to be welcomed as they teach you the lesson of humility and reverence. Running after external things produces all this discontent. That type of desire has no end. Once you become a slave to the senses, they will not leave hold until your death. It is an unquenchable thirst. But I call you to Me and even grant worldly boons, so that you may turn Godward. No avatar has done like this before, going among the masses, counseling them, guiding them, consoling them, uplifting them, directing them along the path of Sathya, Dharma, Shanti, and Prema.

My activities and movements will never be altered whoever may pass whatever opinion on them. I shall not modify My plans for dharmasthapan–the establishment of righteousness–My discourses, or My movements. I have stuck to this determination for many years, and I am engaged in the task for which I have come, i.e., to inculcate faith in the path of prashanti. I shall not stop nor retract a step. Not even the biggest scientist can understand Me by means of his laboratory knowledge. I am always full of bliss whatever may happen. Nothing can come in the way of My smile. That is why I am able to impart joy to you and make your burden lighter.

I never exult when I am extolled, nor shrink when I am reviled. Few have realized My purpose and significance, but I am not worried when things that are not in Me are attributed to Me. Why should I worry? When things that are in Me are mentioned, why should I exult? For Me it is always Yes, yes, yes. If you give up and surrender to the Lord, He will guard you and guide you. The Lord has come just for this very task. He is declaring that He will do so, and that is the very task that brought Him here.

I know the agitations of your heart and its aspirations, but you do not know My heart. I react to the pain that you undergo and to the joy that you feel, for I am in your heart. I am the dweller in the temple of every heart. Do not lose contact and company, for it is only when the lump of coal is in contact with the live ember that it can also become a live ember. Cultivate nearness with Me in the heart and you will be rewarded. Then you, too, will acquire a fraction of the supreme love. This is a great chance. Be confident that you all will be liberated. Know that you are saved. Many hesitate to believe that things will improve, that life will be happy for all and full of joy, and that the golden age will recur. Let Me assure you that this Dharmaswarupa this Divine body has not come in vain.   It will succeed in warding off the crisis that has come upon humanity.''

- SATHYA SAI BABA

DRUG ABUSE

* *More than one-third of American young adults currently use illicit drugs.*
* *Five million Americans currently use cocaine.*
* *The U.S. Surgeon General estimates the number of young people under 18 who are involved regularly with some form of illicit drugs to be in the millions.*

These facts from the American Council for Drug Education are startling. The use of illegal drugs has grown to such proportions that it has become a national crisis.

Drug and alcohol abuse is an illness that has touched countless lives and families in America. It is the unsung war in our country. There is no visible enemy to attack. There is no evidence of the dying, the injured, or bombed-out buildings. This enemy destroys from the inside out. This enemy is self-inflicted and self-destructive.

The victims of this war are men, women, and children. Alcohol and drugs have eaten away their self-respect and destroyed their character. They are not physically dead, but nevertheless they are dying within, a death of degeneration. They become incompetent and lay lame in the arms of an uncaring society.

This illness is like a plague that has spread from child to child, adult to adult. The symptoms are related to apathy. The users lose interest in work, achievement, pride of self, and/ or country. They lose human dignity. They live in a state of depression and confusion when the artificial 'high' has died. Their thoughts and desires are driven by the unfulfilled habit, the need to feel 'high' again.

Sai says, *"Today man is pursuing unrestrained sense cravings. These pursuits drag man's mind into the gutter."*

This war is unsung because it has a stigma–the stigma of shame and failure. Parents, teachers, priests, and ministers often hide the illness when it touches their families, schools, or congregations. To sing out is an announcement to the world that perhaps they have failed.

These people are the character builders, the role models, of our nation. They feel responsible for the decline and decay of character that is self-evident in our country today. No individual, supportive of moral values wants to see the destruction of morality that is associated with drug and alcohol abuse.

As long as we support the habit through silence, greater numbers of people become victims. It is a hidden habit. *"The welfare of the nation ultimately depends upon the quality and nature of the individual. Therefore, reforming the individual is of primary importance. Reforming the individual has two aspects: First, weed out the evil thoughts and bad habits. Second, cultivate good habits."*

Who is responsible for this illness in America? Moms, dads, brothers, sisters, uncles, and aunts–the American family. This excludes no-one. We share this responsibility equally because it is destroying our world family.

"CONDEMN THE WRONG AND EXTOL THE RIGHT AS SOON AS YOU NOTICE EITHER IN YOUR CHILDREN; THAT WILL SETTLE THEM ON THE STRAIGHT PATH."

Drug and alcohol abuse is a plague. It doesn't choose or select its victims. No one is spared because they're a good parent, go to church weekly, attend good schools, or live in a certain location. It spreads to every household. It's like the darkness of night and falls on every home.

My family fell victim to all the deceptions of this illness. My grandfather was an alcoholic. He would drink, go into a wild rage, and the family would admit him to a mental institution. I was always told that grandfather was mentally ill and had a bad case of nerves. For forty years, grandfather's drinking habit was kept secret.

My mother was also a victim. She inherited her father's nervous system. Depression and Mom's inherited nervous system fell victim to tranquilizers and sleeping pills. My mother's doctor was responsible for the start of her drug habit. For the next 25 years it was hidden, and so remained untreated. At the age of 70, I took Mom to a doctor who helped her through withdrawal. It was most difficult and took great courage. I admired her immensely. The next victim was Donna.

This   chapter   and the next are written about   our daughter who got started on drugs at the early age of 11 years.   Some people will agree with our open candid approach but others will feel that this is a personal and private family matter and should be kept quiet.

I   want to explain as best I can why Robert and I wanted   to share this with others.   Alcohol and drug abuse is an illness that spreads to the whole family if one member is a user. It is contagious and creates behavior that emotionally upsets everyone in the household. So if a user is living with family members the problem is multiplied   by the number   in   the   household.   The problem   is   too severe for any human to cope   with therefore in 'Alcoholics Anonymous' they call on a higher power and know that this is their hope and salvation.

If I can bring one person closer to Sai Baba by telling them how very much His Love and Grace protected and guided us through the worst problem in our life, I will have accomplished our purpose in writing this story. Knowing Sai as God and knowing that He is continually watching over Donna made our life bearable. If He can help us so much, He can also help others with severe problems.

Our other motive is prevention, perhaps through sharing our experience another parent becomes more aware and can help their child. Isn't that what our life and experiences are all about? Sai says, ***"Experience, experience, experience".*** He is teaching us to learn through our experiences. I pray that this story will do just that. I want you to know that Donna has taught us more about life, love and God than any other child. We do not blame her nor ourselves for this is our karma and we are simply trying to reach out and help others.

Baba announced His Divinity to us in 1976, and one year later we discovered our daughter's drug habit. She was then thirteen years old. His Divine timing made it possible for us to lean on Him during one of our most difficult experiences in this life. His teachings gave us guidance and strength. His example taught us the meaning of detachment and love-not human love, but Divine love.

"There are two forms of love. One binds you to God. The other binds you to the world. The mind is responsible for either of these states. It is like a lock. If you turn the key to the right, the lock opens. If you turn the key to the left, it gets locked. The heart is the key to the lock of the mind. If you turn the key toward the world, you have attachement (bondage)."

It was Donna's first year at Lindbergh High. She was a freshman. I received a call from one of the counselors saying that Donna was skipping class and hiding in the bathrooms. She was having trouble understanding the freshman academic studies.

Throughout grade school, Donna had been a slow learner. She attended special math and reading classes. Frequently, I would ask Donna's teachers if she had a learning disability. I was always assured that she was simply slow. In high school, Donna was placed in the maintstream of students. Her support system for the slower student was gone. She was intellectually lost. If she asked a question and couldn't grasp the answer, her peers laughed. The classrooms were overcrowded and the students undisciplined. One of the teachers confided in us and openly admitted that he could not control his class because they were so undisciplined. It would be hopeless for a student like Donna to get any special help from him.

We needed to know if Donna had a mental handicap, so we had her tested. The diagnosis was that she had suffered brain damage during the birth, causing learning disabilities. We reported the results of the tests to the freshman principal, who requested that the school district also test Donna. I welcomed the additional testing. Their results confirmed ours.

I had difficulty recognizing Donna's drug habit. Donna's behavior resulting from learning disabilities, covered up the drug taking symptoms because they were also related to learning: shortened attention span, impaired communication skills, reduced ambition, and a drop in the quality of school work.

The school district was very cooperative. Donna had special teachers in her freshman year, and we applied for admission to the vocational training school, Vo-Tech. We were advised that at this special school, the teachers would work with Donna's learning disabilities on a one-to-one basis. If she stayed in the present school system, graduation was a slim possibility. Her chances for graduation at Vo-Tech were very favorable.

That was the good news. The bad news was that only 40 students–20 girls and 20 boys, from a total of about 300 applicants–would be selected. We wanted this opportunity for Donna. I knew it would take a miracle, but I also knew where to ask for one.

Baba tells us to always call on God for His help. <u>God can't answer if we don't call.</u> This petition is only the first step. It is our responsibility to do our utmost to resolve the problem. We are his instruments, his arms and legs. Only when there is nothing further to be done do we surrender the outcome to the Lord. Robert and I applied for her entrance to Vo-Tech, surrendered, and waited for a miracle. She got accepted!

Donna's behavior at home progressed from bad to worse. Her moods would swing from hyper to depression. I asked her if she was taking drugs. She would vehemently deny and accuse–deny any involvement with drugs and accuse me of distrusting her. The more I corrected her behavior, the more offensive she became. I was the person she chose to blame.

When our children are young, they have a protected environment provided in the home with adult supervision. The older they get the less parents can provide protection. The child becomes a teenager who wants freedom from parental authority. They want to date, drive and be their own parent. Their wisdom lacks experience and the knowledge we gain from living. We, parents, take a great risk if we allow our teens to be self-directed. They don't realize it but their life is in danger.

Donna's behavior was unmanageable; I somehow had to learn the truth buried amongst her continuous lies.

She always denied the use of drugs. I became desperate, and searched her room, found marijuana–my answer. When I confronted her with the evidence she denied that it was hers, and said that she was merely keeping it for a friend. She could lie with such assurance, and parents want to believe their children. Who wants to admit their child has a serious problem, has broken the law, or injured another? Parents want only the best for their children, and looking at our child's mistakes automatically requires self analysis. Reluctance or refusal to do the latter is often the barrier that keeps the door closed on the facts. Sai Baba says *"Drugs are deceptive, debilitating, and dangerous, and they have deleterious consequences".*

About this time, a new Sai devotee came to our center, Dr. William Harvey. He was Administrator for NASCO, Narcotics Service Council, which had two facilities,–one an in-house treatment center and the other specialized in counseling. Sai had sent us help through Dr. Harvey, who offered his friendship, understanding, and the services of NASCO. Each week, I took Donna and two of her friends to counseling, but each week they became less interested. The problem was I wanted them to be cured; **they** didn't.

The counseling was a beginning step, a seed planted for a future cure. My desire for Donna's cure was great, but only Donna could turn the key from abuse to non-use. I felt lost. There was no clearly defined course of action. I had to wait, and my helplessness only increased my frustration.

It is painful to watch someone destroying themselves. When it's your own child, the pain is intensified. For a mother, it is unbearable. A mother's life is devoted to caring for the needs of her child and solving their problems. If the child has a bodily injury, one applies soothing medication and love. But how does one help when their child grows-up and doesn't want it? I told Donna, "that a mother had a very special relationship with each child. When a mother shared her body with another person a relationship of closeness was developed. I felt so close to her and more than anything I wanted her life to be filled with happiness. I would always love her and I would always be there for her and I would fight to help her overcome this habit." I would say, "that I know you can give up this habit and even if you no-longer want my help I will storm the door of heaven with my prayers."

I turned to Baba for answers. I observed Him in His role as a parent. He yearns for us to be free of all desires so we can merge with Him, but He is not free to change us until we become ready to receive what He has to offer. We must decide ourself.

I asked myself, "If God can wait patiently for me, why can't I wait patiently for Donna?" What does God do while He is waiting? He gives selfless service to others. His conduct is an example of love. I found my answer in His words and actions. *"Serve in order to heal the agony in your heart."*

I took Swami's advice and began to help in the community. My feelings of helplessness diminished as I reached out to others who were <u>ready</u> to receive. I discovered that the love I shared with them, when returned, multiplied and replenished the emptiness in my heart. I was and still am intensely grateful to my Sai Physician for His home remedy on heart agony, prescribing service to others, which translates into Love.

In the household, money started to disappear. I'm definitely not an accountant. I do my shopping and write checks or pay cash. I don't keep tally of the exact dollars left in my purse. Nor have I had reason to. If I ask you how much money is in your purse or wallet, you most probably would give me a "guessed amount." I occasionally found myself saying that I thought I had another $10 in my purse. The amount Donna took was usually small and more difficult to notice. Most of the time, I would pass it off, thinking that perhaps Robert took it or I had made a mistake.

One day Donna got caught. I had cashed an $80 check and came straight home. There was no mistaking the amount this time. I put my purse on the desk and left the room for a few minutes. That particular day, something prompted me to re-check my purse. Twenty dollars was missing. I looked outside and Donna was walking up the street. I caught up with her, brought her home, and asked her about the money. She denied taking it. Finally, I had to search my own daughter and found the missing money. I can't begin to describe the sadness I felt inside.

My role in this life is wife and mother, not policeman. When the crime that exists on the streets enters your home, as a daily threat, and the thief is your daughter, what do you do?

We had serious talks with her, punished her by taking away privileges, gave her counseling, had her earn the stolen money through her employment etc,. Her jobs were never permanent because she was using drugs and was not reliable. Since she had a learning disability drugs only increased her handicap.

A home should be a place where you can rest from the turmoil and negativity that exists in society. The atmosphere should be somewhat harmonious and filled with love, peace, and understanding. The purpose of our home is to strengthen, renew, refurbish and refresh us so that upon rising each morning, we can face the world with equanimity.

Our home was the opposite. When Donna was home, it was more peaceful outside. She would be high and screaming or depressed and screaming. She would curse and embarrass her younger sister Joan in front of her friends. Joan was always upset over Donna's behavior. Craig wanted to right her wrongs. He would judge her behavior and tell her how to correct it, ending in an argument between them.

"Is it possible for a single individual alone to achieve peace? If there is chaos and unrest all around you, how can you alone have peace? If there is no peace in the home or in the community, how can you have peace? Your peace is dependent on peace in the family, in society, and in the world. You cannot be indifferent to the state of the environment in which you live. One

who wishes to dig a well for pure water will choose a spot far from polluted or saline areas. If you want to achieve peace, you have to see that the atmosphere around you is conducive to peace. This means that you have to cultivate the feeling that your individual peace is intimately related to the peace of the world."

Our home was in a turmoil, Donna was unhappy and would take her feelings out on everyone at home. I prayed for it to become a loving home, filled with peace. I knew this would be a reality someday, but I didn't want to wait–I wanted it now. We live in a Instant Society.

We have instant cameras, instant food, instant news, even instant marriage and divorce. Sai Baba tells us that He can change us instantly, but that it would not be permanent. His method is to change us slowly and permanently. I asked myself what did I want–a fast fix or a permanent one? God needs time to correct, what took time to create. I decided I was prepared to wait.

One night Donna left to go out with several girl friends but never came home. We were extremely worried, stayed awake most of the night, and prayed to Sai for her protection. Early the next morning, I called her friends, who also took drugs. I strongly felt that one of the girls I called was hiding Donna. Her parents were divorced and the mother worked. It was the logical place to hide out for the day. The mother would never know if they attended school or not.

In an effort to prevent me from bringing Donna home, they called the Child Abuse Hot Line phone number and reported Robert and I as child abusers. Teen-agers on drugs will stop at nothing. We were investigated like criminals, and found guilty until proven innocent.

I can certainly understand a teen running away from a parent who abused her. But Robert and I never struck Donna and there was no justification for the phone call. We gave her so much love and understanding. Our image as good parents was being shattered, my mind recalled the delightful little blond curly headed child who used to hug us and love us. Where was that innocent child? Does she still exist underneath all this ugliness? Can drugs trick the user's conscience into believing any behavior is acceptable, as long as it fulfills their needs regardless of who is injured mother, father, sister, brother, lover, or dearest friend? Over and over the same question nagged at my heart.....Why? It's so difficult to accept that one of your children would humiliate, and dishonor you. Nothing seemed to be sacred.

Several days later we were investigated by a 25-year-old case worker. He arrived at our home at the same time as Donna's school bus. As he spoke with both of us, he noticed that Donna had two cigarette burns on her hands. It looked like someone had put their cigarette out on her hands. It made me sick. I ached for the ignorance of this child.

The case investigator sent Donna to her room. He accused me of putting the burns on her hands. I was outraged and vehemently denied it! He had accused me without any facts. He spent the next ten minutes interviewing Donna. When he returned, he admitted that she was at fault, not us. He left with a warning that this report would stay on our records for one year and would be removed only if no other complaints were filed.

I was mad, angry and hurt. I cried out to Baba, "What are you doing? The harder we try to practice your teachings, the more criticism we receive."

Sai Baba has given His devotee's four rules to remove anger. I tried them all. He tells us, " to physically walk away, or lie down, or drink a glass of water, or look at your face in a mirror."

In December 1986, Dr. Jumsai, from Thailand explained the scientific reasons for Baba's four methods of controlling anger.

When angry, we create a strong anger vibration of energy. The longer we stay in this field of energy, the more we will be influenced by it. If we become angry or someone else is angry, we must remove ourselves from the situation immediately.

The second rule is to lie down. When our spine is horizontal, we cannot get angry. When a person is sitting down and gets angry, what happens? You rise to the occasion and express your anger. Lying down prevents the ascent of anger energy.

The third rule is to drink a glass of room-temperature water. Dr. Jumsai told us that when we drink the water, it will bring our body temperature down and dilutes the impact of unwanted chemicals in our blood stream. Also, by drinking water, we restore the balance in our body.

The fourth rule is to look at our face in a mirror the moment we get angry. When we see this ridiculous look on our face, the anger can turn to laughter.

After I calmed down, I realized that I was blaming God for my problems. It's so much easier to blame someone else than oneself. I realized that my ego was associating with the image of being a 'good parent' and that attachment angered me when I was judged as being abusive. It's impossible to hide our ego in the shining face of His Truth. It is not an easy task to look at our ego images, but it is a necessary process if we have self-realization as our goal. We can never become one with our Divine image, God Self, when our little ego is blocking the path that allows the God Self full expression. Be like a hollow reed. *"God is not involved in either rewards or punishment. He only reflects, resounds, and reacts! He is the Eternal Unaffected Witness! You decide your own fate. Do good, be good, you get good in return. Be bad, do bad deeds, you reap bad results. Do not thank or blame God. Thank yourself, blame yourself!"*

Sai Baba tell us that we are the creators and designers of our life. The conditions that exist in our lives are the results of past actions. For every action there is a re-action.

"The sacred Scriptures of this land loudly proclaim that the individual is the architect of his own fate: high or low status in society, luxury or poverty, liberty or bondage. Whatever form the person craves for now while alive in this world, that form he attains after death. Therefore, it is

102

clear that karma decides birth and that the luxury or poverty, the character and attitude, the level of intelligence, the joys and griefs of this life are the earnings gathered during the previous life. The inference, therefore, is inevitable that the next life of the individual will be in consonance with the activities prompted by the level of intelligence which rules the person here and now."

The problems that exist for me in this life, are from my previous births. This knowledge, helped me to understand, that I was not an innocent victim being besieged by an un-merciful God. God's justice is definitely accurate and not left in the hands of a lottery ticket. It is not by chance or a game. It is an accurate ledger, accounting for every entry of revenue, debits, or credits.

Sai Baba tells us how to remove negative karma. *"The consequence of karma can be wiped out through karma, as a thorn which can be removed only by means of another. Do good karma to assuage the pain of the bad karma which you have done and from which you suffer now. The best and the simplest karma is the repetition of the Name of the Lord; be ever engaged in it. It will keep out evil tendencies and wicked thoughts. It will help you radiate love around you."*

In this lifetime, I want to go one step further. I am not interested in acquiring any more karma, not even the good. Sai Baba tells us that the law of karma not only applies to bad actions but also good actions. Therefore, I can return to earth not only to repay bad actions but also receive the awards of my good actions. I want to get off this merry-go-round, the repeated cycle of birth and death. Sai Baba tells us how we can end this ceaseless cycle!

He has given to us a most precious gift, a gemstone of wisdom—the permanent answer to end the cycle of future lives. For the Spiritual seeker it is the most beneficial teaching of Sai Baba, Nishkama karma, - renunciation of the results of our action. Whilst here on earth we must act, so Nishkama karma is the only sure way out of the cycle.

"Surrendering to the Lord is surrendering all thoughts and actions, not wishing for the fruits of the action...doing action because it is one's duty. The act is dedicated to the Lord and the results, therefore, are borne by the Lord. Actions done thus, fruits abandoned at the time of action, such action is free of karma."

RECOVERY

Little by little, over more than three years, Sai Baba prepared Robert and I for the day when we would be confronted with a critical decision.

It was the fall semester of Donna's senior year in school. I drove her to school in the morning because the school buses were on strike. I watched her enter the building and, as I departed, thought to myself that at least I knew she was safe at school.

When I returned to the school in the afternoon to bring her home, she was not there. I inquired, but no-one had seen her. Her teachers had marked her absent for the day. "How could this be," I asked, "since I had brought her there in the morning?" There was no answer to my question.

How foolish the mind, thinking that a place

represents safety.   Only God can protect and be with us at all times.   But the question remained, "Where is she now?" I prayed, "Oh, Baba, please HELP."

I called all of her friends, but again no-one had seen Donna.   Not until late that night did we discover, that Donna had been at her boy friend's house in the evening, but had left at 10:00 p.m.   She then walked to a nearby Pancake House to telephone a girlfriend from school who was baby-sitting.   Donna was supposed to spend the night with the girlfriend – Jane – someone who was unknown to me.   I finally found Jane's home phone number and spoke with her mother.   She replied that her daughter was baby-sitting but did not know where.   She told me she would call me if Donna came home with Jane.

We received no phone call through the night.   In the morning, I again called Jane's mother.   She told me that her daughter had returned home alone, and confirmed that Donna had called Jane from the Pancake House saying that she would hitch a ride and come over.   Donna had not arrived.

A wave of fear rushed through my body.   I was scared. This no longer seemed like a delinquent teen-ager prank, but something much more serious.   I didn't want to think of the possible consequences.   I prayed again: "Oh, Baba, Baba, Baba, HELP!"

I called Donna's school, looking for more facts.   I explained the situation to the principal and asked if she could discover when Donna left school.   I also asked about her friend Jane.   The principal told me she would find the answers and call me back.

After   questioning the teachers and students, the principal learned that Donna was absent again the second day and no one had a clue where she was.   To make matters worse, the principal told me that Jane was a troubled girl and a terrible influence on Donna.   She continued by saying that Jane had   a   very   strong, dominating   personality.   Donna could easily   be persuaded and go along with peer pressure without any personal discrimination. She had a strong need to be accepted.

I   called Robert to come home from work.   We contacted the police who came to our house and took a statement from us but they could do very little at this time. We contacted the Missing Persons' Bureau, and found out that they will not get involved with a case until the person has been missing for 48 hours. I expect the authorities get calls every day, and to them this type of event is purely routine, but to us, it was anything but routine. It was our daughter who was missing. Their support and reassurance was nil.

No wonder parents go crazy. Your child is missing and there is very little that you can do. It is beyond our comprehension. We had to let go and give the problem to God. The only person that can protect and locate Donna was God, so we prayed.   How very grateful we were that we had Sai Baba to lean on and give us hope!

We called the juvenile authorities, where finally, we found a sympathetic ear.   They said they would call Jane and   her mother to confirm their story and alert the local police to keep a surveillance on their house in the hope that Donna might eventually go there. They would be able to observe but not enter.

We prayed and waited. The years of practicing patience helped us in this waiting game. In a time of crisis, you must and can rely on the skills that you have developed through practicing Sai Baba's teachings of detachment and focusing the mind on God, because the mind wants to race into the future projecting all the fearful images of crime that your senses have taken in during your lifetime, rape, murder, kidnap etc. etc. We prayed to Sai Baba for our daughter's safe return. We visualized Donna and surrounded her with Baba's white light of Love energy. Not only did this exercise help Donna, but it kept our minds busy.

It was Friday, time for dinner, and Robert had just come home when the phone rang. It was one of Donna's friends, John. He said, "Mrs. Bruce, I know how worried you must be about Donna. We are too. Mary and I are going to devote the entire evening searching for Donna. We'll check all our local hang-outs and let you know if we find out anything about her whereabouts."

He called the next morning. "Mary and I went to the Pancake House and found a waitress who saw Donna on Thursday night." This verified part of the story. I knew this young man was also a drug user, but I couldn't imagine anyone lying about anything as serious as this. I thanked him and checked the story myself.

The waitress described a girl who came in on Thursday night around 10:30 p.m. to use the phone. She described my daughter's features and clothing. The waitress also observed three vans with male occupants parked in front. She said it was possible that Donna had hitched a ride in one of the vans, but she only remembered her using the phone and leaving. She told me that Donna's friends, who came looking for her last night were upset and the girl was crying. After talking with the waitress, I felt certain that Donna's friends must be telling the truth.

We also received a call from the juvenile case worker who confirmed Jane's and her mother's story. They had not seen Donna. The picture seemed grim. The pieces of the story all appeared to fit. The waiting was agony.

A crisis acquaints us with two kinds of spiritual awareness one's strengths and weaknesses. You can easily determine your level of detachment, by observation. Our growth was obvious but so was our need for improvement. *"When obstacles come, they should be taken as tests. Tests are intended not as punishment, but are given for ascertaining one's fitness for promotion. Frequent tests mean frequent opportunities for promotion. If there is a big time lag between tests, it only means that promotion is not possible for a long time."*

Our years of spiritual practice certainly helped us in this crisis. I recalled the very first time our daughter didn't return home. We barely slept all night. But this time, as strange as it may seem, we slept the entire night. Every night before sleep, we prayed to Baba for her safe return, offering Him our troubled minds and hearts. Night after night, we fell fast asleep. It was a miracle. His gift to us of sleep allowed us to cope with the days.

It was noon on Monday when the four days of waiting came to an end. My eldest daughter Carol was manager of a dress shop in a nearby mall. Donna and Jane casually strolled into Carol's store as if nothing had happened. Carol took her to the back room, questioned her, and some of the story seeped out.

I have given this story in detail because it is an example of the destructive behavior caused by drugs. The following is what really happened.

Donna and Jane left school on Thursday, shortly after I dropped off Donna. They walked off the school campus and spent the day taking drugs. The bus strike gave the girls a perfect cover since absenteeism was high.

Donna spent the evening with her boyfriend, an evening which ended in a quarrel. She walked to the Pancake House, called her friend John, who drove her to the residence where Jane was baby-sitting. Both girls were later driven to Jane's home by the baby's father. Jane's mother sheltered and hid Donna until her arrival at Carol's shop on Monday.

It was an incredible story. How could John, Jane, and her mother tell so many lies. How insensitive they were to us. Donna and Jane lied to Jane's mother. They told her that Robert and I were child abusers. She thought she was protecting Donna. She blindly believed both girls, and lied to the juvenile authorities. Never once did she question the girls or call the police to verify their story. John's behavior was really sick, I thought. He knew exactly where Donna was living and fabricated the entire story of Donna being missing. The waitress had told the truth, and John used her to affirm their lie.

It was difficult for us to believe it all had happened. How could anyone be so inhuman as to allow parents to think that their daughter had been abducted? And how could our daughter agree and participate? The answer was drugs. We were told several years later by one of Donna's counselors that she had experienced blackouts during those days of her absence and recalled very few circumstances. She had no awareness of her behavior nor how it touched our lives. She was blank.

Sai says, *"Today, uncontrolled living habits and unrestrained social behavior are extolled as signs of freedom. It is really only freedom to slide down into the animal behavior from which man has risen."*

While Donna was missing we had consulted with Dr. Soto, a psychiatrist, who specialized in drug abuse cases. In the event that Donna was found, Dr. Soto gave us specific instructions and it helped to have a plan of action to follow. He told us to call the juvenile authorities, who would pick her up and detain her for questioning. He suggested that we leave Donna in the Juvenile Home for one night. We were to call him and he would admit her to St. John's Hospital for drug rehabilitation. We followed his advice.

One of the juvenile case workers called us after interviewing Donna. Robert answered the phone. "Mr. Bruce, this is Ms. Young from the Juvenile Detention Home. We have your daughter Donna here. Mr. Bruce are you sitting down?" She started laughing. "In all my years, of being a detention officer, working with youth, I really thought I had heard it all! But this one's the best. Your daughter says you believe that a fuzzy-haired, black man who wears an orange robe is GOD! You parents have got to be 'OK' but your daughter has a problem!"

We roared with laughter. The Lord knew we needed to laugh. It relieved the pressure. Life is really his leela, his play, so why do we take it so seriously? Robert and I became credible because a black God in an orange robe was incredible! I think Sai spared us from another investigation.

After a month of treatment and therapy, Donna came home with promises of staying clean and dry. We were so happy and hopeful. I honestly believed that this might be the turning point.She joined AA and attended a weekly support group. Donna had to find new drug free friends. We hoped this would happen through AA. It was too big a step for her to take. We screened incoming calls and visitors, but we couldn't patrol her when she left the house. In a few short weeks, it became apparent that Donna was intoxicated with her old friends and habits. How I hurt for my child and didn't know what to do next.

"Spend your time in good company. When we make

an inquiry as to what is the meaning of good company, we will come to understand it by saying that it is friendship with good people. You may ask what is the benefit that we will get out of such good company? Man's good as well as bad features receive their final shape when he mixes with other members of the society. If you spend your time in bad company and wander about the streets like stray dogs, whistling like foxes, you will only be wasting your life. Time wasted is life wasted."

Donna's conduct was self-destructive. Usually through giving love and discipline, you can help your children change their behavior. We tried everything we could with Donna. We talked, shared our love and concern for her, shared our feelings, told her we were confident that she could overcome this problem. Just lean on God and us. We wanted so very much to help her. But nothing seemed to work. Swami had taught us to be far more loving and foregiving than we were in our early years of parenting. I couldn't believe that this Love that flowed from Him did not bring a response from Donna. Why wasn't it working? Swami told us in an interview that she would never listen to me.

Most parents know that they hold one last trump card. When all else fails, we can remove the child from our home. We had never been willing to take this final step because Donna was so young, and we had hoped that our love and caring could help her to correct her behavior. But the only thing that would help Donna correct her behavior was HERSELF and only when she finally desired to change.

It was time for us to remove the safety net and stop

picking up her pieces. It was two weeks before Christmas 1981. Donna had turned eighteen on December 1st. It was obvious that she needed more remedial drug treatment. At the age of eighteen, she was legally an adult, and could no longer be classified "delinquent" and now had to give her own consent to any treatment. Two weeks earlier our course of action would have been different. God was making sure that it was Donna's decision, not ours.

We gave Donna a choice. She must admit herself into another drug treatment center or leave home. How I prayed that we would have the courage to act on our decision.

Robert and I spent two hours one Saturday morning, trying to convince Donna to make the correct choice. We could no longer watch her destroy herself, day after day. It just hurt too much. Donna chose to leave home. We helped her pack and watched her walk away. Words cannot describe what we felt, so I won't even try.

I pleaded with Baba on the inner level, "Don't ever have us do this again." But Baba knew that I would have to say "No" to admittance to our home many times in the future. *Love must be regulated and directed by intelligence and discrimination. Or else it may cause even injury and defeat.* We were learning to give "Tough Love," caring enough to change a loved one's behavior even though you risk losing them.

Three days and nights passed and we heard nothing from Donna. Then she called, asking to come home. Inside I screamed. "Swami, do you hear me, I don't want

114

to do this again." But in my heart I heard Him say, "It's the only way." I knew He was right.

To Donna I said, "No, not unless you go through another drug treatment program." She finally consented. We immediately took her to Weldon Springs Treatment Center for children and youths. It was imperative that we act swiftly. We felt that any delay might heighten our chance of losing Donna or of us weakening. We prayed to Sai and asked him for a sign to reassure us.

We had our sign within the first week. Donna had a group therapy session in the TV room of Weldon Springs. As she entered, Sai Baba's picture was on the TV screen. It was an incredible experience. She thought He only existed in pictures on her parents wall, and now He was on television.

The "Lost Years of Jesus" was being aired, but no-one in St. Louis knew who was responsible for this show. Baba had synchronized the place, time, channel, and His appearance for the very moment that Donna walked into that room. Most of the video portrays Jesus life and Sai Baba appears only in a small portion. God's EXACT timing. We had our sign, but God gave us another to assure our certainty.

Parents are required to attend weekly informational sessions at Weldon Springs. On Sunday when we attended the session, Sai delighted me with his sense of humor. I had told Swami that I'm a bit slow and if He's trying to tell me something to put it on a blackboard and spell it out in black and white. Well, He did!

The instructor of the class rolled a large blackboard

into the room and used it for a film screen. The treatment Center showed a film in which Father Martin gave a lecture on the disease of Drugs and Alcohol. In the film, Father Martin was using a blackboard to illustrate a diagram.

He drew two circles, and in the middle of each circle he wrote the words "hate" and "love." Around the word "love," he drew arrows pointing outward. He said that the qualities of love radiate outward to others – giving, loving, kindness, helping, etc.

Around the word "hate," he drew arrows turning inward. The qualities of hate reflect inward to us – greed, envy, selfishness, and self-pity. He said that depression is nothing more than self-pity, feeling sorry for yourself.

His statement set-off a chain reaction inside of me. I could instantly see myself and how sorry I felt for Rita. Was I creating my own depression? "Is this Your message for me?" I asked Sai within? Then I noticed the blackboards. Not one but two. The film was being shown on a blackboard and Father Martin was writing on a blackboard in the video.

I turned my head and looked at the side wall. There were big letters on the wall made from green construction paper they spelled "R I T A." I couldn't believe my eyes. He not only wrote out the message of my depression caused by self-pity on a blackboard, but just in case I doubted the message, He signed my name to it in big letters for me to see! How did the green letters get on the wall? It was Christmas, the letters spelled out

"MERRY CHRISTMAS." All the letters fell off the wall except "R I T A", hidden in the word CH**RIST**MA**S**!

Sai Baba is always telling us that He is omnipresent, guiding us, teaching us, and protecting us. He is with everyone. But we must have the eyes to see him, the ears to listen, and a heart that is open to God. *"When the magnet does not attract the needle, the fault lies in the dirt that covers up the needle."*

We learn from our mistakes. Donna couldn't cope with the influence of her friends. If she was released and returned home, it was certain that she would make the same mistakes. Her chances for success would improve if we could remove her from her friends.

I spent a lot of time trying to learn what to do next. I spoke with people who had experience and could guide me. I was told that Minneapolis is known for their progressive treatment centers and halfway houses and excellent drug-recovery programs. Donna's chance of recovery would be much greater if she was given a new start. We wanted her to have every possible chance to recover no matter what the expense in terms of our love, time or money. But I wondered how could we get her to go there? I didn't have a clue and left that in the hands of Sai Baba.

We prayed and by some miracle Donna agreed to go. We drove to Minneapolis and left her in the hands of an excellent halfway house program which included daily AA meetings. A halfway houses means living halfway between a treatment center and on your own. You go to work, but you still have the support of an institution.

117

They teach you how to adjust to society and live drug-free. We again felt hopeful. I was never so happy than to get her there safely. I was afraid of weakening and turning back because it was so hard to leave her alone with no family.

But success was not going to be as easy as we had believed. Donna was expelled from one house and ran away from the other two. I was afraid we were going to run out of halfway houses before she decided to take it seriously. But by the grace of God, she eventually decided to obey the house rules and follow the AA program.

Donna needed self-confidence and was afraid of failing at a job. It was so important to Donna and to us that she improved her self concept. We praised her at every opportunity and we were very aware when we communicated to avoid criticism and put-down statements. We wanted her to realize her wonderful potential and we were so willing to help her. But she just never would respond to us. I think that was one of the most difficult adjustments we had to make, **not** to have any expectations. We had to surrender to God. We certainly didn't understand what was happening.

Baba started her recovery very slowly. Her first job was working in the cafeteria of the halfway house itself. Then she worked at the front desk, using some of her secretarial skills. Eventually she earned enough confidence to seek a part-time job outside. She worked at numerous part-time jobs. Four years later, Donna was able to work forty hours a week, supporting herself.

It was a wonderful step forward, and she really liked working! We were so proud of her.

It takes time for the Lord to change our behavior. Patience is the precious friendly virtue that allows us to wait until changes are made. Sai says, *"Patience is all the strength that man needs."* And was ours being tested!

Some years later, we were told by one of Donna's counselors that she experienced drugs at the young age of eleven. It took three years before we noticed her behavior changing. Her habit progressed to daily dependence on marijuana, amphetamines, alcohol, and the hallucinogen LSD. I didn't have a clue that she was using anything other than alcohol and marijuana.

This is why it is so important that our schools become drug free and they are not. It's an open season for drugs in the very heartland of our children's world, their school. This institution teaches prevention and discourages drugs. Nevertheless, they are hidden in lockers, in pockets, purses, and under the desks, waiting to slip into the hand of a student who may some day loose his/her life. Why can't our children at least be safe in their daily environment? If my child got those drugs from friends at school and I was not aware and I stayed home every day to greet her......isn't it logical that it could happen to yours?

Sai tells us, *"The future of the country depends upon the condition and quality of the students. Students may be described as the very roots of the nation. Therefore, we must pour the water of the divine force into the very roots. Students may also be compared to the creepers bearing flowers. If we allow these creepers to grow as they please, they grow in a wild and disorderly manner without beauty and symmetry. Therefore, we must prune each creeper so that its shape may be beautiful and it may not grow in a wild fashion without any beauty. The beauty of life depends upon our good habits. The period of student days is so sacred and most important in life. So the students must be disciplined in their minds and habits and must fill their minds with pure thoughts and try to enforce and put into practice all those good thoughts in day-to-day life and in their day-to-day activities. Only then can they attain the right stage of development."*

A better quality of life is much more than the material standard of living. Our children need a safe environment to live in. How can a country as intelligent as ours be so stupid as to put our children's lives in jeopardy? Don't they understand that the future of our country is our children?

I have told our story to help others. It was an extremely difficult experience. My heart goes out to all parents and children today, all of whom are at risk. I cannot know the horror of peer pressure which our children encounter. I can only imagine. My childhood was free of the sort of temptations that occur daily in their lives. I can only feel their restlessness, confusion, agony and pain, and long to help them.

Our story is duplicated in many households across our nation. When you tuck in your young children at night, or watch them playing innocently you may wonder,

"Are they going to be a future Donna?" I pray they are not.

If someone in your family needs help. . .get it!

If someone in your family needs to be informed. . .do it!

If your child's behavior is suspicious. . .investigate it!

If your neighborhood is promoting prevention...support it!

Remember. . . .if you hide addiction. . .IT STAYS!

MARRIAGE

I had been married for twenty years when I first met Sai Baba and had enough experiences in my marriage to know that what He said is indeed the Truth. Sometimes I thought if I had known Swami's teachings at the beginning of my marriage maybe some of my mistakes could have been prevented. But as Swami tells us *"Past Is Past: Live In The Present."* He also says we must not try; but DO.

In the United States, the experience of divorce is widespread. The sacred, holy institution of marriage, given to man by God, is being defaced and defamed. One out of every two marriages ends in divorce, and one million marriages break up each year. Believe it or not, the divorce rate is higher among re-marriages, and forty-five per cent of all marriages are re-marriages. The family seems to be dissolving into singles.*

122

Divorce was uncommon during my parents' generation. It rarely happened especially to my parents friends who were all devout Roman Catholics. It's not that they were free from marital problems but the emphasis was on staying married. Either they would resolve the problems or learn to live with them. At that time, they rarely had a choice, since women were not financially independent.

There was a sexual revolution for women in the 1960's because of the freedom provided by birth control pills. I remember the lengthy discussions I had with my friends in those years, each of us searching our conscience trying to justify the use of the contraceptive pill. I never fully realized the drastic effect this pill would have on social morals. Today, many of our youth use it like a one-a-day vitamin, and it is now accepted behavior. The whole sexual revolution has threatened our system of marriage, and increased the divorce rate.

Baba says, *"Artificial means of preventing conception will promote licentiousness and bring down on the country bestial promiscuity. Those who encourage these dangerous tactics should instead encourage sense control and self-restraint. Restraint and service were methods advocated in the Scriptures by sages who knew the calamities that are the consequence of irresponsible fatherhood or frustrated motherhood."*

There was another revolution sweeping my country and creating conflict in my life, in the fifties and sixties. The financial revolution gave many women freedom to earn a salary in the market place. They were encouraged

123

to shift from the traditional role of wife and mother to a career. This financial freedom also jolted the marriage system.

The Women's Liberation Movement told us that we should put our career first. They said, "make something of yourself." Women who stayed home to care for the family were regarded as "Obsolete Failures!" Baba has told us, *"Passion makes women aggressively bold, adventurous, and desirous of freedom from restraint. The day when passion is accepted as a mark of womanhood, it will mark the beginning of the end of femininity."*

I struggled with the feeling of worthlessness. Even though inside I knew the value of motherhood, that image was being rejected by society. My peers were upgrading their skills, returning to college, looking for employment, becoming 'marketable'. It all sounded so exciting, new, and glamorous. Let's face it the repetitive tasks of cleaning, cooking, washing, ironing etc. leaves the image of homemaker looking dreary, dull and dumb.

Homemaking has had the image of being a thankless job for generations. There are very few ego perks. How many times have I wanted to quit, find some escape from the awesome responsibility of housekeeping and child rearing. Women were being given the chance to do just that, to flee from the nest, and they flocked to make the most of these chances.

My girlfriends would call and say, "You have so much talent, why are you wasting it at home?" This kind of encouragement created dual desire in me, career woman and housewife. Even as I sit hear today I can relive the old impulse of excitement vs. boredom. No-one in their right mind would select housework over a career unless there is a higher motive, a deeper reason, a lifelong commitment, something beyond the surface of the job descriptions. Sri Sathya Sai Baba taught me the true role of a woman and gave me the reason to believe in myself even though society still places greater value on women who work in the market-place instead of the home.

"Motherhood is the most precious gift of God. Mothers are the makers of a nation's fortune or misfortune, for they shape the sinews of its soul. Those sinews are toughened by two lessons they should teach: fear of sin and fondness for virtue. Both these are based on faith in God being the inner motivator of all. If you want to know how advanced a nation is, study the mothers. Are they free from fear and anxiety, are they full of love towards all, are they trained in fortitude and virtue? If you like to imbibe the glory of a culture, watch the mothers, rocking the cradles, feeding, fostering, teaching, and fondling the babies. As the mother, so the progress of the nation, as the mother, so the sweetness of the culture".

But before Swami entered my life, I succumbed to the desire of working outside my home which simply added another job to my already overtaxed body and mind. I now had a career in real-estate, plus wife, housekeeper and mother. I felt like a marathon runner, trying to reach the finishing line, each day in each job. I had more work allotted to me than humanly possible to achieve. I realized that I couldn't do it all. I had expected more help from my husband and children. That was pure fantasy!

"When women leave their homes for jobs, where are the housewives to do the household chores? When both husband and wife go to their offices, where are the mothers to look after the children? When the mothers go to school to teach other children, who will teach their own children? Even if the monetary position is eased, other difficulties arise in the home. In trying to secure comforts, the office-seeker achieves only an emptiness at home."

I would come home from work tired and stressed out from the job, trying to greet my children with an attitude of interest and patience. They waited for me to return home with their overdue need for attention, each one trying to outdo the others seeking parental approval in all the sibling rivalry games. The fighting, criticism, yelling, homework, and chauffeuring schedules etc. had to be organized. All four of them would blast me as I came through the door, each with their own demands.

My eldest daughter tells me she gives the children "Quality Time" when she comes home from work. This term means that the time she spends with her children after work is quality. It didn't work for me, after a day full of demands, faced with the demands of the family, many times my mood was anything but quality.

In respect to child rearing, Baba teaches; *"Mothers must assume this responsibility and not throw it on child caretakers. The child who is brought up by the child carers loses an essential fertilizer for growth-love. The child is denied the most health-giving vitamin=love."*

126

Shortly after I began my career, I found Swami. He abruptly put a stop to my career with my illness of inner-ear unbalance. How appropriate the diagnosis, every area of my life was unbalanced. So dear Swami intervened, and helped me by sitting me still long enough to rethink my values. In the many months of quiet rest, He taught me the true worth of motherhood. It was the first time that my head and heart were united. The guilt of neglecting the home and children pulled on my heart but my head was repeating the sounds of women's liberation. Strange but true, Swami liberated me from the women's liberation movement.

The American family over the past three decades has changed radically. There is basically little if any family structure. Divorce and single parenting seem to be replacing marriage. Who are the innocent victims? Our children. One out of every third child will watch their parents separate. The break-up is almost as traumatic as death. I've watched my friends and my children's friends go through a divorce. The pain and turmoil they suffered rendered us full of feelings of helplessness. The break-up is like a death. There is no-way to repair the emotional damage to the parents and children.

We have lost sight of the value of marriage, which is the medium God uses for teaching and training mankind morality, manners, discipline, achieving harmony with others, parenting, devotion etc. If the family unit disintegrates how can God instruct newborn souls?

"The Mother is held as the object of affectionate reverence in Indian culture. She is the mistress of the

house, the earliest teacher of the child, the person who lovingly transmits the culture of this ancient land to its heirs in their most formative years. The mother and the father are the first examples in social behavior that the child sees before it and learns to imitate. They teach adoration of God and surrender to the Highest; they represent equanimity and love before the watchful and receptive eyes of the children. So they have to be inspired to take their share in the spiritual awakening...... Tolerance and humility have to be promoted in the rising generation through the promotion of spiritual discipline among the mothers. Everyone has a mother as the source of his life and body. So the mother has to be strong in mind and body, ripe in culture and character, sanctified by holy thoughts and steeped in love and dedication. Good mothers make a good nation. Mothers have to be repositories of detachment, discipline and devotion."

Divorce is not the answer. It has been tried now for long enough, and found to be ineffective. Men and women alike prefer to marry and want a successful marriage. We seek the companionship, support, love and emotional security that can exist in marriage. None of us wants the emotional horror of divorce, nor do we wish to make victims of our children.

The institution of marriage is not at fault, according to Swami's principles it's our matrimonial conduct that needs correction. Marriage comes from God. It is the first institution that God gave to man. It is the very same process that God uses in creation. Shiva and Shakthi, matter and energy, unite to create our world.

MARRIAGE

Marriage is as old as creation; it displays in a practical way the philosophy of life, the joining together of two to unite as one. Male and female, two complementaries, join together to create another in their own likeness or 'image'. This institution of marriage is the form or formal structure through which our responsibility for our own creations can be exercised. God has thus allowed us to share in creation through the institution of marriage.

In the book, "Divine Memories of Sathya Sai Baba, Diana Baskin, the author, shares her wedding ceremony given by Sai Baba. Swami says: *"Before marriage, he is half body. Before marriage, she is half body. Lady is always left side. Right side is gent's. The gent's body is always the right side of the wife. Now you have only one body. In Indian philosophy or custom this is called ardhangi. (Ardha means half.) Wife before marriage is only ardhangi, half body. Now the left side is joined with the right side and you are full body.*

"In the future, husband's troubles are wife's troubles and wife's troubles become the husband's. It is like, if one part of the body is paralyzed, the other part of the body feels the paralysis. And so, your wife must feel your pains and you must feel her pains. Both of your pains are removed by Swami. Both of you have Swami. Both husband should help wife and wife should help husband.

Sometimes, it is natural for you to have anger, ego, temper, tension. You must have adjustment and understanding. "First you must understand each other. After that, adjustment will be easy. First understanding.

Second adjustment. Ninety percent of people try adjustment first. This is the wrong way around. **First understanding.***"*

During our original marriage ceremony, we also were told that each of us are now a half, and must unite as one. But no-where in the ceremony were we told what a difficult job this is to achieve. I'm sure we would have been divorced, if Swami hadn't intervened. Sathya Sai Baba saved our marriage. It's not that we didn't try every available tool on earth that we could find, but while I searched for a solution, only God could change the consciousness of Robert, to realize he was also a contributor to that solution. We were married 34 years ago, Robert and I were young and very much in love. I believed he was perfect. I could see no faults, swept up in the romance of our meeting. As the married years clicked by, I wondered what happened to the love we had before marriage. Years later I would find my answer.

Sai Baba tells us that the ego must give up its body identity in order to merge with our real identity, the God within. For us marriage has been the laboratory where the "ego melt down" takes place. Sometimes I think nothing short of self-realization can achieve perfect selfless love in marriage.

In order for two to join as one, each of the two must sacrifice their ego desire to merge. Now we've all heard that opposites attract and when they come together they rub the wrong way and cause friction. Friction creates heat, heat creates energy, and energy melts the ego. Thus the ego-melt down!

To name a few examples: Robert wants to watch the

football game on television, I want to watch a movie......I want to diet and not cook dinner, he wants dinner.....I want to use the car for shopping, he wants to clean it......He offers my services to baby sit without asking me.....I want him to bathe the baby and he wants to read the paper.....someone's ego must melt down. The larger the family the more opportunities for the melt down! I'm convinced that whoever selects your marriage partner God, parents, or you, their behavior will be opposite to yours, perfectly designed to aggravate, irritate, and snag your ego. One day I realized that if God joined us with what we thought the 'perfect' marriage partner, there would be no growth. And if I look at marriage through God's eyes, I see Him as a mischief maker whose main objective is guiding us to Him. When we are happy and content with the outside world we usually forget God. Adversity forces us to turn towards Him.

As the honeymoon faded into the passing years, the reality of our opposite personalities emerged. So many times I wanted to go in one direction and Robert in the opposite. Once in a while we agreed but more frequently we did not. God surely had a plan when He created opposites, because we balance each other. Through understanding and awareness we were able to see that Robert's skills and virtues, were sometimes my weakest and vice versa. After our ego or self-importance became less, we began observing and learning from each other. This process did not happen over-night nor did we change instantly, but I assure you that we had many opportunities to practice and eventually with the grace of Sai Baba all things are possible.

To explain this, here is an example: The wife (me) likes to talk; the husband is more silent. Each skill helps to balance the relationship. If both were silent, then there would be no communication. If both liked to talk, who would listen? So you observe each other, communicate with each other and develop what each of you lacks. The ideal goal is to attain both skills and use them with discrimination and in a balanced way.

Our marriage of 'opposites' was no exception to the rule. It was a good example of what I am referring to. I lived in the county (suburbs); he the inner city. My family was very religious; his hardly had any. Discipline was enforced in my home; his had none. His father did the cooking; my mother did ours. His mother played with the children; mine did the chores for hers. I am the oldest; he is the youngest. I am a slave to time; he loses it. He communicates through actions; I communicate through words. He is show; I am tell. He speaks indirectly: I speak directly. He spoils the children; I discipline them. "Closeness" for me is communication, talking to share ideas and thoughts; "being there" is enough for him. I stayed home all day and had no adult interaction; he left and had too much interaction. After work, I wanted to go out; he wanted to stay home, etc. By now you are probably nodding your head in agreement. Isn't it funny how the cards are so stacked against being united?

Our differences caused marital conflicts. My father did not help with any chores at home, and much of his free time was spent playing sports with his friends. I got married with the intention that my husband was going to help with the chores and children and include me in his free time. Now, on the other hand, Robert's father did most of the chores after work. Robert's hidden expectation was that he was not going to cook and clean like his father did; he was going to have fun like Mom. Can you imagine, how many times we tripped over those differences every day?!!!!

Another example...... communication. Robert and I discussed cleaning the garage. It's dirty and cluttered with "old junk." I ask him while cleaning the garage if he will throw out the excess junk, that has been sitting there unused for years. As he remains silent and doesn't disagree openly, I assume he is agreeing. Since he speaks indirectly and doesn't like verbal conflict, he remains silent. The junk remains! His actions communicate his thoughts, and create conflict. This is just a sampling of what each of us experience in marriage to varying degrees. When we're newly wed, the differences are not as obvious, but with years of living together, the unknown becomes known. I wonder if that's what they mean by the saying, "Love is blind."

After ten years of marriage, we had a stockpile of hurts, resentments and rejections, and our marriage had a major crisis. It's like the over crowded garage where too much junk has accumulated. It begins to overflow beyond the boundaries. Our containers could no longer contain or suppress our feelings, so one day we exploded with anger towards one another. I call it the "big bang" theory of marriage, its a point when we reach our maximum emotional pain level and this crisis forces a change. For some it's a cleansing, sharing, and changing their relationship, and for others, separation.

For us, it was the beginning of our creating a more meaningful marriage and relationship. Through intense searching for love, looking at our faults and injustices towards each other, we made the "act of contrition." It is a prayer I learned as a child, but says exactly what we needed to tell God and each other. 'Oh, My God, I am heartily sorry for having offended thee, I detest my sins, and firmly resolve never to commit them again.'

We had to change our behavior and that does not happen overnight. Thirty-four years later, and we are still working towards a more loving relationship; but now we can laugh more at ourselves. It is only through God's Grace that our marriage has survived. Our relationship touched upon almost every conceivable problem that could exist between a man and a woman who were united to be one in the holy state of matrimony. Matrimony is first; uniting is years later!

The uniting process calls for a strong commitment from both marriage partners, but remember opposites attract, and one partner usually wants to make a commitment, and the other does not. What do you do? Pray for Swami's help and, if possible, push and pull the opposing partner along the way.

Baba tells us that the woman is responsible for her husband's devotion to God. I have always wondered why women were more motivated than men in this process? One reason: it's our nature. I'm not implying that it's always women and never men who are motivated but it has been our experience that it is mostly the female who first sees the need and actively works for change.

To summarize this chapter on marriage, let's pretend that each of us on our marriage day are brand new cars. We drive our new cars home. The wife drives her own, and the husband his own. Every-time we have a personality conflict, we bump into each other and dent our cars. When we persist in believing that our way is right, and resist communication, understanding, and change even though it is hurting our marriage partner, we dent the cars. Accidents also occur when we express our anger, jealousy, or hatred.

Depending on the intensitity of opposites, the amount of damage and length of time varies, but one day you may discover that your car has some damage, has been in a wreck, or is totaled. When any of these happen, we can be injured. Some cars can go to the work shop for repair and some are beyond repair, demolished. . .divorced.

Repairs are costly in terms of expense, time, and labor. I can only take my car in for repair, not others. Each of us must decide to drive our own car in the shop for repair. This is essential before any work can begin. So, each marriage partner must express a desire and make a commitment.

I don't know why some cars can be repaired and

others cannot. I am certain that Sai Baba wants us to work at hammering out the dents. Today, so many people just dent a fender then junk the whole car, or sell it to someone else, - damaged.

Is it worth taking your car to the repair shop? **YES!** I believe so.

It has taken a long time to iron out our dents. We have been in and out of many repair shops. We lost fenders, rearranged the engine, removed doors, stripped the interior, and somewhere, somehow we ended up with only one car! Half of it is his car and half is mine. If we get a dent, now we know, we're damaging OUR car. It has been in and out of so many shops, we know all about our car and just where the engine misses and needs special attention. So when it's in for repair, the time is less and expense rare. It's much easier to have a tune-up than a complete overhaul!

Sai says, *"You are really loving yourself, for there is only you in everyone. He is I. Whoever you injure, it is you that suffer; whosoever you cheat, it is you that are cheated. There are no others. You are all living cells in the body of God. You are yourself, God."*

Sai Baba has elevated the role and image of marriage and parenthood to its rightful position, a place of honor. The goals He has set before us to achieve are a lifetime challenge. It is not a mediocre task; it requires a lifestyle of virtue. We can be examples to others who marry. It is exciting and worthwhile to realize that we, as men and women in marriage can grow in our love for God, and share together that love with each other.

Marriage is a sacred sadhana. It is God's playground for the spiritual aspirant to practice multiple dimensions of bhakthi. It is His laboratory for testing our "ego" power to determine if it is used for God or self.

As we enter our house of marriage, we are crossing the threshold of God's House:

The kitchen is for preparing food; we gather recipes of ancient spiritual knowledge.

The Dining room is the place were we eat and digest the spiritual food and its nourishment becomes wisdom.

The Living room is were we live God's laws.

The Bathroom is the place were we cleanse ourself from daily impurities, with love and forgiveness.

The Bedroom is the private place were we awaken the sleeping God within us.

Each room is electrically wired for light and energy.

The energy of God is the Light of His Divine Love.

"Expansion is the essence of Love. When a lamp is lit from another, there are two where there was but one. The first one did not stop emitting light. You can light a million lamps from one; yet, the first will not suffer a jot! Love too is like this. Share it with a million; it will still be as bright as when it was alone."

God has given us this great institution of marriage

to realize and experience His love. Within these walls all family members can safely minimize the ego and turn to God, instead of the world. It is the place where all souls who are born and reborn live and develop. The responsibility of evolving man from animal behavior to divine behavior with each new generation rests in the lap of each husband and wife. There could be no loftier task on this earth than to shape and change the nature of another human being, to achieve self-realization.

"Children are the crops growing in the fields, to yield the harvest on which the nation has to sustain itself. They are the pillars on which the foundation of the nation's future is built. They are the roots of the national tree, which has to give the fruits of work, worship and wisdom to the next generation".

As devotees of Sai Baba, how can we help Him? We can restore marriage to its place of honor in each of our respective countries by making our own home the temple of God. We can live in love with each other, not quarreling with one another. We can let the sweetness of God's love flow from our lips and spread joy and happiness to all the members of our household.

We can be an example of truth, right conduct, peace, love and non-violence. Virtues are taught by practice, not precept, to our children. And we must remember that love can only find expression through service that begins in your home.

Sai says, *"The home is the temple where each member of the family is a moving temple and is nurtured and nourished. The mother is the high priestess of this House of God. Humility is the incense with which the house is filled. Reverence is the lamp that is lit, with love as the oil and faith as the wick. Spend the years of your lives dedicating them for such worship in the homes that you have and will found."*

"Start the day with love, fill the day with Love and end the day with Love. That is the Way To God."

Note: Statements in this chapter about marriage and the family in the United States are based on statistics given in "After the Sexual Revolution," an ABC documentary.

HOLY WEEK

At the start of our third trip to visit Sai Baba there were many delays even before we left the ground. Travel in India provides long lessons in PATIENCE because there are countless hours of waiting in lines for almost everything. I chuckled to myself, wondering if Sai was warning us that "this trip will call for greater patience due to excessive delays."

On our second trip in the private interview, Swami had asked *"How is your health, Madam?"*

It seems that time and space do not exist for Sai Baba. He continued the conversation on my health right where we had left off, two years ago, in our first interview.

"It is a little better," I had replied.

"You have much confusion worrying about the future. What to do or not to do? Whether to stay or go? Stay; Go.

140

Stay; Go, Stay; Go," He chanted.

Robert asked, "Swami should we stay in St. Louis?"

"Yes," said Baba, *"You stay in St. Louis, and I will give you much blessing."* There is no way that Sai would have known about our obsession to leave St. Louis, other than through His Divine Omnipresence.

We had lived just one block from the ocean in Australia, over ten years ago. It spoiled us and created in us a huge desire to return to the coast.

In the past two years, there had been three job opportunities for Robert on the West Coast. Two were unsolicited. On each of these occasions, we even looked for a home because the job seemed so certain. Then suddenly the offer disappeared as quickly as it occurred. We thought we were moving, "Go". . .then we found out we were not "Stay!" This happened three times since our last visit to Sai Baba. How appropriate are Sai's choice of words, go..... stay.... spoken three times!

We had felt great disappointment after each job refusal. We realized our test was to become unattached to living in any one type of place. It might have been an easy test for someone else, but for us our desire to live near the ocean was great. Swami was holding both of our hands, and His beautiful glowing face radiated love as He looked into our eyes, guiding us with His wisdom, helping us to overcome our attachments.

Robert asked, "Swami, it is our 25th Wedding Anniversary, will you please marry us and make rings?"

141

We thought since this is our anniversary it must be the right time. Swami, began moving His fingers up and down each of our ring fingers on the right hand, as if to be measuring up the size.

"Yes", He said, *"I will marry you before you leave and make rings. When do you leave?"*

Robert answered, "January 15."

Baba says, *"Before you go. After marriage, you will have much peace and health, you will be very blessed."* It was music to my ears.

We joined the rest of the group. As Baba distributed Vibhuthi, He re-affirmed to me His promise. *"Do not worry, Madam, I will marry you before you leave."*

As the days of our second trip came to a close, the marriage did not happen. My last darshan, I pleaded to Baba, from my heart. "Oh, Baba, please," I said as He came near to me. *"Oh, Baba, please"*, He mimicked, while offering me His hands. I held them so tightly that Robert saw Swami shaking His hands to free them from my clasp. I returned home with His all consuming love, a firm grip on His hands, and a promise of a future marriage.

I had a secret request, a contingency clause, attached to this "re-marriage" ceremony. In my heart I had asked Swami to re-marry us only when Robert and I had concluded our marriage karma, which had been considerable. Therefore, I realized that I was returning home with more karma to work-off.

I asked myself, why did Swami feel my ring finger on the right hand, instead of my left which is the correct hand for wedding rings in our culture. I didn't understand. Later I discovered that the correct ring finger in the Indian culture is the right hand.

A few months after we had arrived home, I was using an electric knife, it slipped from my hand and very stupidly I tried to catch it. My ring finger on my RIGHT hand was badly cut. The knife diagonally went through my finger just below the knuckle. At the hospital the doctor remarked that he couldn't believe that the tendon was not severed. Then I remembered Sai's finger moving up and down my right hand ring finger. It was Thursday (Sai's day). The finger was stitched and bandaged just in time for us to attend Bhajans and give thanks, that evening.

On March 25, 1983, we arrived safely in Bangalore. We heard from our cab driver, Bala Gopal, that Swami was in Brindavan; and if we left immediately, we could have His morning darshan. We were so anxious to see Sai Baba, again. We longed for this moment many times during the past two years.

We know that Sai is always with us because He is the God within, the Divine Resident. But His physical form is a visual reminder of our true nature, unconditional love, which we know exists but is seldom evident. When we see God in human form; we experience His treasure chest of infinite everlasting wealth, which sparkles and shines with a brilliance that blinds us to pain, and opens our hearts to receive His riches of Selfless Divine love. While we are in His presence, He heals and strengthens us. He recharges our batteries with love and arms us with knowledge and the courage to slay the giants of desire that live within our mind.

"He who has the least desire is the richest man in the world.   He who is filled with desires is the poorest man in the world."

A hush came over the crowd as He appeared.   The familiar small   figure in orange, repeating the same monotonous schedule.   How sick and tired we humans would be of His daily routine.   Only God   can give continuous selfless love to all around Him, as He does.

I had a mala (garland) of flowers to offer Sai as a token of thanks for all the help and blessings He had given us since our last visit.   Baba   blessed our flower mala, and gave me the opportunity to express our thanks.

After   darshan,   we met some friends who remarked that Sai Baba was not granting any interviews to foreigners at   Brindavan.   This   was   a pattern that had been established for   many   months, now.   I never place too much importance on the interpretations of Sai's actions because He is so unpredictable. He can change anything at any time. We also learned that Sai Baba was going to demolish His old residence here and build a new one on the same site.   He was in the process of moving some of his belongings to another residence on the Brindavan Campus.

We   were very glad to be back here.   His darshans were long and sweet. Now Palm Sunday arrived, marking the beginning of Holy week. In the past, Holy week had been a time of spiritual significance for us. I wondered if this week would have a hidden surprise.

We arrived for early-morning Nagasankirtan, singing God's Holy Name in the streets of Kadugodi, the near-by village and returned to receive the last balcony darshan from the old residence. I found a quiet place to meditate. Unexpectedly, I found myself faced with so many feelings that I had put aside that year, relating to our daughter, Donna. I had had some tough decisions to make. I had to ignore my feelings or I would have lost my objectivity.

"The secret of happiness is not in doing what one likes to do, but in liking what one has to do."

My mother's instinct felt immensely sorry for her, and I had just wanted to hold and rock her soothing her, as I did when she was a child. But she was no longer a child. Her long-ago childhood innocence had been seduced by society to feed her senses. I had to face this reality even though it was painful. We all like to recall what is pleasant, but sorrow, pain, resentment, conflict and disgrace are unpleasant. Swami helped me open my reservoir of feelings, washing them as they surfaced. Perhaps early-morning Nagasankirtan had purified my inner self. Every act we perform has dual benefits, both outer and inner.

A day later, Robert wrote a note to Sai. Baba took the note and read it. In a loud voice Swami said, *"monkey mind."*

Robert asked, "Should I meditate to get rid of it?"

Swami said, *"No meditation, Go!"* As Robert walked

145

toward the Brindavan residence, I followed. As we sat outside the interview room waiting for Sai, I was curious. What had Baba said to Robert? We were too far apart to speak, so I had to wait, patiently.

Swami returned from darshan and called us both into the interview room. He closed the door, and motioned for us to sit at His feet. It was our marriage judgment day. Since there are no secrets kept from God, He knew everything about our marriage that had happened. His love and compassion drew us closer to Him than ever before.

Sai Said, *"How is Prema or Love to be cultivated? It can be done through two methods: 1. Consider always the faults of others, however big, to be insignificant and negligible, consider your faults to be big and feel sad and repentant. By these means, you acquire the qualities of brotherliness and forbearance. 2. Whatever you do, with yourself or with others, do it, remembering that God is omnipresent. He sees and hears and knows everything. Whatever you speak, remember that God hears every word; discriminate between the true and the false and speak only the truth; whatever you do, discriminate between right and wrong and do only the right. Endeavor every moment to be aware of the omnipotence of God."*

When Swami finished talking about us He reached down and took the pictures I was holding of our children. He commented on two of the children.

Our son Craig wanted Baba to give him permission to marry a girlfriend. Swami advised us to tell Craig not to marry this girl, but to wait. Swami will bless him. Baba gave us a message for Craig about the girl that we did not understand, but Craig did, as soon as he received the message.

This was the first time Sai Baba has spoken to us about Donna. He offered us some very helpful guidance. We were not certain that Donna was capable of supporting herself, so from time to time we sent her financial help when she requested it. Baba told us that she was able to care for herself. We should not send her money, and when she was married, we could help more. He told us that He would give her a job.

It was an immediate release from the past nine years of doubt and anxiety. We often wondered if she could overcome her insecure self-image. We knew if she could get a job and keep it, her self-confidence would increase. Swami answered our prayers. He gave her a job, and we gave no more financial help.

I bent over to kiss His hand and foot in gratitude for His gift of help and love. The words swelled from my heart, and I cried out, "I love you, Baba,"

Swami looked at me with such sweetness and said, *"I love you, I Love You, I LOVE YOU VERY MUCH."* Each time He repeated the phrase, the expression and tone in His voice slowed down and intensified. I have never heard words spoken with such depth of feeling. It seemed superhuman. I believed it to be God's voice projecting His magnanimous love for mankind.

I knew immediately that His message of love was not only for me but for all mankind, so I share this experience with you, because SAI BABA is great, not Rita. His love is no greater for one than the other. He makes each of us feel special, but in truth none is more special than the other. His love for each and every one is equal.

I read once a quote from Swami, which said that His love for the most devout devotee is no greater than His love for the worst sinner. It made me cry. His love surpasses all human understanding. You can take this experience and make it yours if you wish. Just close your eyes, and listen to His voice within you saying "I love you." When you open your eyes remember that the only thing Swami asks for from us, is our love.

Then Swami's hand moved in a circle and He filled my hands and Robert's with Vibhuthi. I have never seen so much coming directly from His hand. He patted my head and said, *"I will heal you."* His hand then revolved in another circle. This time he materialized a beautiful silver medal and placed it in my hand. It is the face of Sai Baba deeply engraved in a 3D dimension on one side with the symbol of OM etched on the back.

We left the interview room in a daze and slowly walked across the darshan area to our cab. By now everyone had left, and we were grateful for the silence. The interview was overwhelming, and we returned to our hotel, trying to digest the spiritual food He had given to us on this Holy day.

The following morning, the Brindavan Residence, including the interview room, was being torn down. We may have been the last foreigners to receive an interview in that old building. But for us it was a sign that our

148

sins spoken of on that day in the little room were destroyed and shattered with the hammer of His Divine Will. It seemed that this Holy week would not pass uneventfully.

On Holy Thursday, I wrote Sai a note saying, "Yesterday you told us of our problems but spoke nothing of a cure, please take this note and give me padnamaskar, only if you promise complete removal. He walked directly to me, took the note, gave me a big smile and I kissed His feet. My gratitude was too deep for words.

"The mind wills, yearns, prompts, and insists on effort and action. This process is called sankalpa."

No matter how severe your problem, or how deep the roots of sankalpa, His power of love will heal the mind and remove the cause.

I recounted this because I want every one to have hope. No need to give up; stick with Sai. He has helped us through some difficult karma. When the karma was over, He helped us to remove it, sometimes sooner, and healed the wounds it caused. The words of Martin Luther King come into my memory - "Free at last, Free at last, Free at Last!"

On Good Friday, one of the devotees told us about a shop owner on Commercial Street in Bangalore who had beautiful carvings. She knew that Robert and I loved carvings of wood and ivory. The devotee said that the owner of the shop would be happy to share their beauty with us.

We went and admired the carvings. The workmanship

was so fine and delicate; the designs so intricate. I thought of the many hours of labor and patience working together to create from raw materials these art objects of exquisite beauty. I was really impressed, with the concept of "labor = results". Knowing full well that this same concept could pertain to Robert and I.

One of the last objects we saw was a carving in ivory of Shiva. Robert asked me to try the necklace on. It was very beautiful, and became a gift from him to me. The owner wrapped the necklace in a band of cotton before he tied the outer paper. It felt like pillow stuffing. I noted the unusual wrapping.

On Holy Saturday, Robert brought the necklace to darshan for Swami to bless. Swami raised His hand and with a very hard blow hit the wrapped necklace and said, *"I Bless!"* The thick cotton wrapping was a protection for the necklace. I wear the necklace frequently, because Swami blessed it.

In our next interview Sai pointed to the necklace and asked me, *"Who is this?"*

I replied, "Shiva."

"And where does Shiva live?" He asked.

"In our hearts," I feebly responded.

"No" said Baba. *"Shiva is everywhere."*

Shiva is one of the three aspects of God in the Hindu Trinity. Brahma is the creator, Vishnu is the protector and preserver, and Shiva is the destroyer of all evil. God creates, preserves the good, and destroys

150

the bad. It appears that Sai was bestowing Shiva's blessing on us. Sai's actions strengthened my hope for a cure of my illness.

There was a strong rumor that Sai Baba was leaving for Hyderabad on Easter Sunday night. Devotees were buying tickets to join Sai on the airplane. After inquiring in my heart, I felt that we were to follow also. There were hours of waiting before we purchased our tickets at the Indian Airlines office. The flight was to leave at 6:30 p.m.

Evening darshan was over and there was no indication that Sai Baba was leaving for Hyderabad, but we couldn't wait any longer if we were going to make the flight. We boarded the plane, but still there was no sign of Sai. I thought how irrational our behavior seemed, but it certainly indicated the strength of our desire to be with Him.

We had heard that Sai is usually the last passenger to board, just minutes before take-off. Nervously, I kept checking my watch it read 6:20. . . 6:25 and still no Sai. I looked around and all the other devotees seemed to be restless, stretching their necks to see. I began to doubt, and wondered if this wasn't one big mistake.

Someone spoke in a whisper look, LOOK, then almost shouting "IT'S SWAMI'S CAR!" The gold cadillac swiftly drove across the airport field. Oh! I couldn't believe my eyes. Soon my anxiety melted into joy! It was Easter Sunday and "We would fly, in the sky, with Sai." I could stretch the point and say, "maybe it was a modern-day resurrection!!"

151

Baba teaches us to stay calm, keep the emotions in balance. We must witness and detach. One look at Swami and I felt like dancing in the aisles of the airplane.

What a perfect view we had of Baba! We purchased first-class seats, thinking that was where Sai would sit. Wrong! Sai sat in tourist class, the first seat next to the door. Baba is an example of humility, God sitting in a tourist seat while I was in first class was absolutely absurd but it became our good fortune. We were five rows in front of Sai, sitting on the end seats in the middle section. All I needed to do was turn my head, and I could see His sweet face.

I had a perfect view. I thought, I must be discreet. "How often can I turn my head to take a peak?" I didn't want to stare. Even God needs privacy, I guessed.

In Hyderabad, we heard that Swami went directly to His temple called the 'Sivam' and we followed. The devotees of Hyderbad gave Baba an overwhelming reception. Afterwards we realized it was late, and we needed to find a hotel. Robert and I were not experienced travelers in India, so I sent an SOS to Sai Baba, asking if He would send us a girl I knew from the States or someone who was an experienced traveler to help us.

When we arrived at the hotel, guess who was also arriving? The girl I'd mentally asked Swami for. She said, "I cannot understand why the taxi driver took me to this hotel; it is not the one I requested." She appeared frustrated with the driver. I leaned over to tell her "it's my fault that you're here. I asked Sai to send you."

The following day was Monday, April 4th. We rose

early to attend Nagarsankirtan and the early-morning Suprabhatam darshan, from Bhagavan. Afterwards, Robert and I ate breakfast and took a walk around the Shivam grounds. Crowds of people had amassed during our absence.

As I sat down for darshan I realized that I was so far back. I looked up and an Indian lady was motioning me to come closer. I moved forward. As soon as I sat down, my friend came towards me. She said, "I have a front-row seat and there is enough room for you." I could hardly believe the grace of Sai Baba, caring for my every wish in such a way.

Robert was sitting directly across from me in the front row. It was summer, the heat and sun were sweltering, and the crowds of devotees filled the enclosed grounds and flowed into the streets.

In all of this excitement, we had never inquired as to the purpose of Sai's visit to Hyderabad. While sitting in darshan, Robert noticed that the cornerstone of the Sivam Temple was inscribed with that day's date, April 4, 1973. It was the tenth anniversary celebration of the "Sivam" and it was also Robert's BIRTHDAY. This date, he was told is a very auspicious day for Shiva. There can be no doubt that this was a 'Shiva trip' for us. Shiva was being introduced to us, and I know our love for Him would expand in the coming years.

April 4th became a memorable day for Robert and I. During Darshan Swami gave us Padnamaskar and filled not only our hearts but all the hearts of everyone there. In His love for the many, many devotees, Baba stepped

153

onto a ledge on the stone wall that separated us from the people in the street to give them His darshan. Every step He takes is a step of compassion and love for us.

"God is no stony-hearted despot. He is compassion. He draws you near and grants you consolation and courage."

We spent the entire day at the Sivam, catching glimpses of Sai darshan. He inaugurated the new buildings constructed in the 'Sivam' compound for carrying on service and educational activities of the State Samithi. After darshan, sweets from Baba were distributed as prasadam, or blessed food.

In the evening, Swami gave His Divine discourse on the different types of bhakthi. He said, *"There are four kinds of worship. The first kind of worship is undertaken whenever one is in trouble or distress, then God is forgotten after relief is obtained. The second kind of worship is carried on by the worshiper seeking the good things of life from the deity he worships without depending on others. The third type of worshiper offers worship for the sake of others, praying for the welfare of all and holding to the belief that his welfare is bound up with the welfare of all. The fourth kind, which is the highest form of worship, is worship done in a spirit of complete surrender to the Divine and dedicating all actions to the service of the Divine. This is also known as ananiya Bhakthi."*

His discourse was a call for greater love and surrender from all devotees. He asked us to give service to the people with the greatest hardship, seeing them as God. He ended His discourse, sitting on the edge of the stage, as if to get as close to us as possible. His Love poured forth as He sang and swayed in rhythm to the song called Sai Bhajana. It is interpreted as follows:

"It is not possible to achieve peace and happiness without chanting and reciting the sweet name of Lord Sai.

It is not possible to gain bliss without worshipping Lord Hari. It is not possible to get liberation without love and devotion and detachment.

It is not possible to attain Nirvana or Mukti or Liberation without worshipping the Noble Teacher.

It is not possible to attain Samadhi or union with God, without recitation of the name of the Lord and meditation.

It is not possible to attain supreme knowledge, without a desire to realize God.

No act can be a good act, unless it is done with mercy and righteousness.

There is nobody whom we can call our own, except God.

There is no Lord, except the Supreme Lord of Lords, LORD SAI NATH."

My friend had arranged for us to spend the night with an Indian family who were to meet us at a devotee's house, across the street from the Sivam. It was very late and our day had started at 3:30 a.m. I was exhausted. We waited and the people did not come. We tried to call a taxi, and the 'phone was dead. By now, the Sivam crowd had gone. There were no taxis or rickshaws, but Robert walked down the street. Not knowing what to do, he sent a mental prayer to Baba for help. A young man on a scooter offered to give Robert a ride to the top of the hill, to a busier street, in the hope of flagging down a car.

The Sivam is quite far from town. Robert waited, a car approached, stopped, and a man got out. Since the man did not speak English, Robert tried to explain our need for a hotel. The young man nodded his head when Robert mentioned the name of a hotel. Then he pointed in the direction of the temple and repeated 'Sivam.' The man did not understand, so Robert showed him where to go. Our friend, Robert and I put our suitcases in this car.

The man seemed to be in a trance. We drove a long way. We finally passed a hotel, with a name I was given earlier by a devotee, it had good accommodation and was reasonably priced. It was the hotel I wanted, but I had not been able to pronounce the name. Baba rescued us again!

The next morning at darshan Robert was given Sai Baba's schedule for the week. He was spending two days in Hyderabad, then travelling to Vijayawada, Guntur, Eluru, Kovur, and Rajahmundry. There were only ten days left before we had to leave for the U.S. so we decided to follow Baba if it was His will.

In between the day's devotional activities and Sai darshan we tried to book a plane ticket to Vijayawada.

The flight was wait-listed and my friend, Robert, and I were numbers 8, 9, and 10 on the wait list. We could only hope, and pray, and arrive early at the airport and wait for a seat.

Robert and I rose early and arrived at the airport by 5:00 a.m., hopeful that we would get a seat. Apparently, our friend went back to the ticket agent at 5:00 p.m. the previous night and got a ticket. I knew she was a good experienced traveler, but not that good!!

The flight was due to depart at 6:30 a.m. Soon other devotees arrived and many wanted a seat. When the ticket counter opened, we were told that the capacity of the plane was forty-eight and there were NO available seats. The agent told us to turn in our wait-list tickets and he would refund our money. We declined and asked to hold them in case seats become available. He again stated there were no more seats on that flight.

You can envision that scene. Some devotees were traveling with Sai Baba and had their tickets. Then there were many other devotees who wished to join Swami and had no seats. The devotee politics began by non-ticket holders asking Baba's selected devotees who were going with Him for help to secure them a ticket.

That morning, I had woken with a fever, felt sick and wondered if it was Sai's will for us to stay, rather than follow. But we both wished to go and decided not to give up. It must be Baba's decision, not ours. We waited in silence, only this time my mantra changed to "Swami, can we come with you?" We were now told that we were wait listed numbers 3 and 4, but were told again,

157

no seats available.

It was finally 6:30 a.m. The flight was due to depart. It had been a long hour and a half. The ticket agent called number one and gave him a seat. At 6:35, the agent called #2 and gave him a seat. Both were businessmen. What a pity not devotees, I thought. The man again repeated his motto, no available seats. It's now 6:40, and the ticket agent called "3 & 4." Oh God, it's us! The plane is ready to leave, they say we must hurry. I felt like a kid who had just won a prize at the fair. No-one including myself, would ever have guessed that I felt sick and had a fever as I ran across the field....

Swami was already on board. As I passed, I expressed our thanks. He smiled and said, *"Yes, Yes,"* gesturing as if it was nothing. The stewardess took our boarding passes. We had the two seats directly in front of Swami. There were two male passengers already in those seats. Sai motioned to us and said, *"Find seats elsewhere."*

We were so happy to be on the plane that they could have put us in with the luggage. We had the last two seats available on that flight.

All that rush to go nowhere! It was so hot, the sweat was pouring from our faces. We sat on the plane for 30 minutes with no air-conditioning, in fact, very little air. Then the Captain announced that the flight was delayed until 8:30 a.m. because of poor visibility, fog at Vijayawada. We all deboarded. What a leela!

At 8:30 a.m., we tried again. Eventually, we landed at a place called Gannavaram and drove to Vijayawada by taxi. Baba was to inaugurate the new Sai Mandir there. Crowds of people were waiting for His darshan. The next stop was Guntur.

The May, 1983 Sanathana Sarathi reported these events: "Undeterred by the heat and dust of an Andhra summer, devotees in their thousands greeted Swami everywhere, happy to catch a glimpse of Bhagavan, touch His feet or the hem of His robe, or to listen to His discourse. Swami inaugurated the new temple at Guntur, built in granite in the traditional Indian style, and saw the rural development work being carried on in the West Godavari district by the Sai Seva Samithi."

We arrived in Guntur about forty-five minutes after Sai Baba. Traffic congestion was great, and we had to park a good distance from the new mandir. It was almost noon, the sun was scorching, and I still had my fever. Swami was addressing a crowd of 50,000 devotees when we reached the New Mandir. There was no way to get near enough to see Baba or be shaded by the tarpaulin erected to shelter devotees. Robert asked if we could enter the small courtyard directly in front of the new mandir. It was shaded and there was water for drinking. I have never been as thirsty as I was on that trip. The sweat rolled off my body and needed to be replenished.

In Sai's discourse He said, *"Give up hatred and develop self-sacrifice. It is out of Love that all of you have*

159

assembled here. It is out of Love that I have come such a long way. The tie that binds us is Love. You have built this mandir at great expense. Why have you done it? If God can be worshipped as the Formless Absolute, it may be asked, where is the need for a mandir? But worship of the Formless Brahman is not possible for everybody. As long as you have a body, you need a temple for worship. The lawyer reminds you of legal aid. The temple reminds you of divine help. The body is the tabernacle of the Divine. Our duty is to go to the temple to worship God."

As Swami returned from the discourse, the devotees in the courtyard formed a line to receive His darshan before He entered the new mandir. I was standing very close to the mandir door and the crowds were wild. Some of the people were trying to climb the fence that enclosed the courtyard and the guards were trying to remove them. There were no lady seva dals in this area. As Swami approached me, He looked like the calm in the middle of a storm of people, trying to push in on him. Discipline had gone. Since I am large, I stretched my arms as far as possible, holding back as many ladies as I could saying, "Nay, Nay, Nay, poor Swami." Baba heard and looked up with surprise. The new Mandir door was opened and shut very quickly, and Baba was almost pushed through the opening by the anxious male seva dals who were protecting Him. Swami stayed in Guntur for several hours. It was the first time I had experienced a moving, undisciplined crowd. It was frightening. We waited till most of the people dispersed. Someone had taken Robert's sandals, and the long walk back to the taxi in bare feet on hot, hot ground had him dancing a jig. We were tired, hot, hungry, and thirsty. Isn't it true, when Swami is no longer in view that our attention goes right back to the body?

We had had a diet of pop and fruit, trying to take in fluids, but we still felt dehydrated, and my fever wasn't helping matters. As we passed the Krishna River, it looked cool and inviting. My friend suggested that we go for a dip. In India, I am told, the ladies go in the water fully clothed. It was not the time for me to be prim, so I went in.

We prayed to Lord Krishna to cleanse us of our sins, and fill our pores with His life-giving water. Robert declared that the Krishna River saved our life, I questioned which life - physical, spiritual, or both?

We felt one hundred percent better, our clothing was soaked, but dried very quickly in the heat. We found an air-conditioned restaurant, had lunch, and a rest. We felt Swami's presence all the way.

Feeling rejuvenated, we proceeded to Rajahmundry. It was night before we reached a hotel. Rajahmundry is a small town, and the best hotel in town was filthy. I got out my bottle of Shaklee's Germicide, cleaned the bathroom, and removed the bugs we found in the bed. Too tired to think, we went to sleep.

In the morning we found a note under our door from our helpful friend, who had decided to leave for

Bangalore.   Swami sent us someone else.   Robert met Baba's photographer, Burzis, in the lobby, and he got Sai's schedule for the day. How can one explain all this flow of help, other than Divinity?

Sai   Baba had   arrived   in Rajahmundry at His school about 9 p.m., and was welcomed by many devotees. Perhaps, when we can provide this kind of love and devotion to Sai Baba in the U.S., then He will come there. In one of the villages that Sai visited there was a gathering of 75,000 devotees, and He   blessed   them with a discourse.   This was rough rural country. I wondered where all the people came from and how far they had had to walk?

Bhagavan inaugurated a new hostel for the students at 8 a.m.and proceeded to the auditorium to address the students and staff.   Swami's   love poured out on His children. In His discourse, Sai said, *"Education should be a preparation for the good life, in the service of society and for Self-realization.   The aim of   Sai educational institutions is to reform the educational system in such a way that the students develop respect for Indian   culture and learn to live a life of sacrifice and dedication."*

During Bhagavan's evening discourse, the electricity went out.   It cast darkness on the 50,000 in attendance and   silenced the   microphone.   The crowd became restless, Sai Baba returned to the mike and His voice was heard even though there was **no** power. In the darkness, He calmed and lulled the people into returning to their seats with a Bhajan that was heard over the speakers!

Sai Baba was using GOD POWER! Sometimes, we devotees, see so many miracles from Baba that one begins to take them for granted. But imagine if this happened to the U. S. President. It would make headline's in every newspaper around the globe.

My husband was in the wings of the stage where Sai Baba sat. He witnessed the miracle, and had a small story of his own to tell. Lying beside Robert, on stage was an ill man who Swami allowed to be near Him. The fans were keeping this man cool but when they stopped he became very uncomfortable. Robert remembered the handiwipes he had been carrying around, not using, and took them from his shoulder bag. The handiwipes were wet and cool for the old man.

What is so remarkable, is that the Lord uses all our possessions, time, and abilities to the fullest, when we give them to Him. No thing escapes His Omnipresence. It is especially noticeable with physical objects that are brought from foreign countries and cannot be purchased in India.

The power was restored one hour later, although the discourse was not continued, the message He gave to us that night was not spoken in words. He taught us that His power is greater than any on earth. His compassion and love for us comes before anything else, and His voice will guide us and protect us in our time of need.

The next morning, we were hopeful that we could follow Baba to the Vijayawada airport, but we missed His departure from the school grounds. As we started across the bridge over the Godavari River, we saw Sai's four motorcycle escorts. They told us, "He is visiting a village, stay right where you are, then you can follow His motorcade." Within a few minutes, Sai's car passes, and we were seventh in the line of cars behind. We were so delighted!

Baba's car stopped, and we all got out. One of Sai's aides came to us and asked if we had a cup they could borrow. He sees me take it off the thermos. "Do you have water?" he asked. "Sai is thirsty." Our thermos was half filled with ashram water from yesterday. To stretch our supply, Robert had added a bottle of soda water, before we left.

We gladly offered the thermos for Baba. But we were puzzled. Where was Baba's water? The two passengers traveling with us, had seen the devotees packing large thermoses and picnic baskets full of food and drink for the journey, into the cars traveling with Sai Baba.

Baba's aide returned. "What is in the water?" He asked. Sai tasted and said *"soda water"* and refused to drink it. Robert explained, and I wished our water was pure enough for Sai to drink. We later learned that the car with food and drink had gone ahead. Therefore, the leela of using ours.

We stopped in Elru, a small town. Swami was visiting

a Dr. Rao. We were ushered to a seat on the porch and offered cold water and a soft drink. We could hear the sound of Swami's voice in the background. He was meeting with devotees. It was so nice to be close to Him. I felt like a child sheltered under the wings of the Universal Mother Hen.

The sign that Baba was leaving, was given, and we lined up with the others. We were right next to the door; and as I was basking in the joy of this good fortune, an aide approached and told us, "Baba wants you to go outside the gate."

"What did we do wrong?" was my first thought. Were we being banished? Once outside the gate, I closed my eyes to (go inside) to inquire. He told me to return to the car. We were completely unaware of the large crowd that had formed as we waited for Sai. If we had not obeyed him, we would never have been able to get to our car in time to join the motorcade. Tears filled my eyes when I realized that Sai Baba took time from His busy schedule to remember us on the porch.

The journey resumed but was eventually stopped by a passing train. Sai's car left, but the rest of us remained. After the train passed, we decided to go ahead of the motorcade because there was only one hour left before the plane departed. Swami, did not need to check-in, but we did, so we must hurry.

When we boarded the plane, Sai was already on board. As we passed His seat, Swami asked, *Are you going to Puttaparthi?*

"Yes" said Robert and asked, "When are you going, Swami?" We had to move because we were blocking the aisle and could not hear His answer.

I wrote Swami a note and slipped in the picture of my oldest daughter and her family. Since Swami did not comment in the interview, I thought I would try again.

I gave Sai the note and said, "My daughter is having many problems. Can you please help her?"

He read the note, looked at the picture, and said, *"I'll talk with you in Brindavan."* *"Are you going to Prasanthi?"*

"Yes, Swami, when?"

"Day after tomorrow," He replied. I returned to my seat, and told Robert that there must be some reason Sai wanted us to go with Him to Prasanthi, because He just asked me again. Since we had only a few days left before returning home, Swami was making sure we followed Him to Prasanthi.

We returned to the airport early afternoon because we were tired. Our flight was running late and delayed for another four hours. The omen in St. Louis, of excessive delays, had certainly come true. We waited eight hours altogether in the airport.

We were both feeling exhausted from the week's activities. I knew under normal circumstance it would have been impossible for me to keep up because my health was poor. God's Grace had kept me going.

166

Finally the agony of waiting was forgotten as we sat on the plane with Sai, who looked as fresh as a rose bud, though the rest of us all looked wilted. Baba gave darshan to the pilots and stewardess and materialized Vibhuthi for them. We were in the same seats returning and enjoyed the same view. In our hearts, we thanked Sai for taking us with Him.

I was extremely impressed with Sai Baba's endless hours of dedication to mankind. He readily endured all discomfort. He attended to the smallest needs with the same love and care as to the larger ones. He never tired of giving. The multitudes of people who gathered to see Him reminded me of His earthly mission. How easy it was to forget that He is here to raise the consciousness of our world. It was so easy to slip into I-ness, and narrow vision, instead of the expanded vision of Sai, serving others.

I yearned to give Baba a gift, in thanksgiving for this trip, but what do you give God, who has everything? Swami, in His great wisdom and foresight, tells us the gift to give God.

In 1982, in His Birthday Discourse, Sai told us the most precious gift that we can give Him is to love and serve our fellow-men. *"You can feel that you have given Swami a proper gift only when you love your fellow-men, take a share of their sufferings, and engage yourselves in fruitfully serving them. That is the only gift I wish for. The present to be given to God is pure, steady and selfless love.*

"Rich people and people in power will have plenty of servants. But the distressed, the poverty-stricken, and those who suffer have no one to serve them. Go to such people and be their freind, their kith and kin, their closest well-wishers, let them welcome you as such. If you pour spirituality into the ears of those who are tortured by hunger, it will not be assimilated. First, quench the hunger.

Give them God in the form of food.

Give them God in the form of clothes.

Give God in the form of peace to those who are afflicted with anxiety.

Give God in the form of medicine to those who are suffering from ill-health.

Give God in whatever form will assuage fear, pain and sorrow.

"It is only after this is done that spirituality can soak into the heart. If you act contrariwise, instead of spiritual feelings, you will be promoting atheism itself."

Sai Baba's mission is to build a great mountain of selfless serving love to help those in need, and He needs many hands to do it. The type of job, big or small, makes no difference. But it is important that we do help to the fullest of our capacity and spread His love to all. If we all deposit the soil, of selfless love in the same manner, God will have the biggest mountain of love the earth has ever witnessed. We must watch carefully that our egos do not build their own little mountain, accomplishing nothing. Only when we join together as one united hand, placing the soil of love in the same selfless manner to needy people, will the mountain of love grow.

ATMIC WEDDING

Baba was going to spend several days in Bangalore, before he returned to Prasanthi. We were to depart for the U.S. on April 14. Since Sai had asked us to come with him, to Prasanthi we asked His permission to extend our stay three more days and we changed our tickets.

This morning at darshan Baba again asked Robert. *"Are you going to Prasanthi?"* "Yes Swami. We will leave when you do," Robert replied. Sai left after darshan. We were still curious about Swami asking us to go with Him. We didn't have a clue as to why.

There was a big celebration at the Prasanthi Nilayam ashram. It was Yugadi, the Hindu New Year. We were told that it was a very auspicious New Year because there were three different districts, three different New Year dates, converging at that time. But that New

Year, they fell on the same day, the three dates coincided, something which has not happened for two hundred and fifty years.

In His discourse Bhagavan said, *"Fill your minds with fortitude, patience, truth, and peace and make them blossom so that they may scatter the fragrance of divinity. This is my New Year message for you all. Get rid of evil habits and cultivate purity of thought, word, and deed. Constant repetition of the sacred name of the Lord is the means for achieving purity."*

We had been looking for a picture of Sai Baba for our center, and we wanted Him to bless and sign it. I selected one picture, but every time I took it to darshan, He avoided me. I concluded this was not the picture that He wanted us to use. We kept looking. On New Year's Day, we heard of a photographer in the ashram who sold Baba's pictures, Mr. Padmanaban. We chose a beautiful black and white picture from his selection.

The following day, at evening darshan, Swami called us for an interview, along with fourteen Indian devotees. Swami made me Vibhuthi, and asked, *"Are you fighting with him?"* He looked at Robert and asked, *"Are you fighting with her?"*

"Yes, Swami, sometimes."

Baba does not want married couples to fight. He is firm about this, and His standards are far more severe than mine were. 'Fighting' to Baba is a cross look or a raised tone of voice. One day in meditation Sai told me, "Speak with sweet speech, sweet as amrith!"

Baba was very happy, talking and joking with everyone. He materialized a little gold medal, two gold Hindu Gods, one gold ring with an emerald stone, and a japamala of white milky stones. After seeing Sai's ability to materialize, it no longer seemed unusual but had become expected behavior. The truly awesome miracle that He performs, is transforming us, even though all previous attempts have been failures.

The most desired gift for devotees is His boundless love. We crave it. I was aware of my great good fortune to be there with Him, and I was also aware of the hunger of those devotee's in the darshan lines who long for an opportunity to be close to His Form. I said to Baba, "All those people waiting outside want Your love."

He raised His hands and said *"What can I do? Love is my form."*

It was our turn for a private interview. As we went through the doorway to the interview room Robert put his hand on my arm in a helping gesture. Swami tapped his hand and said, *"Don't touch."*

We knelt at His feet, and Robert asked, "Will you marry us?"

And I added my personal request and said, "Is the karma for us over?"

"Yes" said Baba, *"I will bless."* He looked at me and said, *"Do you want to marry him?"*

"Yes, Baba."

Again He asked, *"Are you sure you want to marry him?"*

172

"Yes, Baba"

He repeated the question again, for the third time, I answered once more. Swami took our left hands and pulled our ring fingers together. This time it was the correct hand for our culture. He said that He would make us rings.

Swami then asked, *"What is tomorrow's date?"*

"Saturday", said Robert.

Baba replied, *"Sunday morning is much better. Marriage at eight or eight thirty."*

"Can we invite some friends?" I asked.

"No," said Swami, *"don't tell anyone."*

"Do you have your camera," asked Sai, looking at Robert.

"Swami," I asked, "would you like to have the camera?"

"Yes," He said, *"for the school boys. Latest model, you know,"* quips Baba. He told us to bring it on Sunday. We asked Him to sign our picture for the center.

Again He replied, *"Bring it on Sunday."*

We returned to the outer room until Swami finished the interviews. Then He reached for His little basket of Vibhuthi packets signaling the close of the interview, and gave each of us a fresh supply. I so very much wished that Catherine Bracey could attend our marriage . I asked Swami and got no reply. I again asked, He answered, *"Whatever you wish, Madam."*

I kissed His feet and He said, *"Don't worry, I will see you on Sunday morning."* I'd heard those words before

173

and wondered if it would really happen this time.

Robert asked, "Can we have a message for the Mid-West Conference?"

"Yes, My life is My Message," said Sai.

Robert tried again. "Swami, can we have your handkerchief for the conference devotees?" He took it off the chair and placed it in Robert's hand.

This time I prepared for the marriage ceremony with caution. If it doesn't happen, my disappointment would not be as great as last time. I told Catherine the good news that Sai granted my wish that she attend our wedding.

On Sunday morning, Robert and I were nervous as we were dressing for the marriage ceremony. I removed from my suitcase a white sari with gold trim to wear on this occasion. I purchased the sari fifteen years ago in Fiji on our trip home from Australia. It looked like wedding material to me and I thought that someday one of my daughters would use it, never realizing, at the time, that it would be mine.

April in Prasanthi is so hot, and my anxiety was not helping. My sari was polyester, a synthetic heat conductor, certainly not appropriate for that time of year. There wasn't a dry place on my face to apply make-up. I left my room feeling like a wilted flower, certainly not a new bloom. How appropriate, I thought, after thirty years of marriage–my blooms have indeed withered!

Catherine and I arrived just before darshan and sat

along the wall. As Sai passed us, He gave not a glance, ignoring us all the way. Inside, I said "You're not fooling me, you know we're here. Is this the day?"

Good grief, it happened! Robert walked up to the veranda. Catherine and I rose trying not to look too conspicuous, but indeed we were. Catherine was so well-known by the residents and I was in a sari with the flashy gold trim.

Sai walked past me, smiled and chuckled, putting me at ease, but then He caught me off guard. He returned and told Catherine, *"I don't want you out here"* and gestured for her to leave. Oh, how my heart sank, as I watched her walk back across the sand. It must be my fault, but what did I do wrong? There was no time to analyze my behavior because Sai was ushering us into the interview room.

As I entered, Swami makes me some more Vibhuthi. After Swami sat down, He started to scold the woman in front of me. I felt uncomfortable with His Shiva form. Next, His attention focused on us. He asked so sweetly, *"Marriage day? How long have you been together?"*

"We've know each other for thirty years," said Robert. Sai Baba talked about marriages in the United States. He said, *"One year they come with one wife, the next year with a new one. Swami never knows from year to year who they are bringing. It's very bad."* He then asked Robert and I if we would accept each other in marriage. He motioned for us to come to His side. He materialized a ring for me and asked Robert to put it on. Robert picked up my hand. Again, Baba patted Robert's hand and said, *"Don't touch."* That's twice. I feel someday there will be a third time.

Baba took my left hand and gave the ring to Robert. Now said Swami "put the ring on." It stuck a little. Swami said, *"I make the right size; it will fit."* His hand circled again and He asked me to put on Robert's new ring. His ring is quite beautiful compared to mine. I thought Swami would make us duplicate rings but ours are so different.

My monkey mind starts its siege of jealousy. Every time I had thought about a ring from Sai, I wanted it to be in gold, with a stone. I didn't want a silver ring with a stone. Guess, what I got? A silver ring with a smoky gold stone.

To add fuel to my disappointment, Baba materialized a gold ring with a large sparkling green stone that looks like a green diamond for Robert. Perfect color for a case of jealousy. I was green with envy! I wanted a ring like his.

Sai gestured for us to go into the private interview room. His actions are playing havoc with my desires. I desired friends. He married us in the outer room with strangers. Had He hooked my "ego!"

When we got inside, Baba was so sweet. *"Very happy"* He said. Robert asked "When can we come back?" Sai told us, *"You are always welcome, anytime; this is your home. I have given you an apartment, for a marriage gift. It will be ready in one year."* What a wonderful surprise!

Swami signed the picture for our center and one for us–a keepsake of our wedding day. He blessed the candy we had brought as prasad and tossed a piece in each of our laps. He asked me, *"Where did you get your sari?"* I start to explain. He replied, *"I know, I know."* He told Robert that He will give me a wedding sari and to come after bhajans to pick it up. Swami blessed us and said, *"You will have health, wealth, happiness, and liberation."* He patted my head and tapped Robert's shoulder and jaw.

After our marriage, Swami gave interviews to the rest of the devotees with us. My thoughts distracted me. "Why are our wedding rings different?", I asked myself? "Why is his prettier than mine? Why did he get the ring I want? - - after all, I did more to make this marriage work than he did." Can you imagine sitting in front of Sai with this garbage going through your mind? I reminded myself that this was the day I had been wishing for. Was this insane jealousy over this ring going to spoil it all?

I felt so terrible and small. How could I be jealous of this man I know and love so well? Instead of rejoicing at his good fortune, my ego was destroying it. Swami had given me so much, why am I looking for more? Where is my gratitude? Finally, I put my ego to death. "Go get stuffed," I told it! "You're not going to ruin my beautiful day."

After bhajans, Robert waited, but Swami sent no sari. I felt that since my thoughts were anything but saintly, perhaps this is Baba's way of acknowledging it. Robert went to Mr. Kutumba Rao and asked about the sari. He said, "Swami gave me strict orders not to be disturbed until 3 p.m. I will ask Swami then."

We intended to leave at noon, but our taxi sharing passengers readily agreed to wait for us. The time was needed for us to rest and collect ourselves. I found Catherine and told her how sorry I was. She is a blessed soul and weathers the moment of embarrassment with quiet dignity. After I came home, I reviewed my notes to see if I could find my error.

It read in black and white. "I ask again, if Catherine can come and He replies, "Whatever you wish, madam." Oh, I sighed. It is not His wish, but mine. My ego tripped so badly. Why am I so persistent in having my own way? How many times did God have to tell me "NO" in one day? I apologized to Sai and sent Catherine a letter telling her how sorry I was for the mistake.

One of the passengers who was sharing our taxi came to our room at 3 p.m. and said that Mr. Kutumba Rao had left Swami's room with a package under his arm. Robert went to the accommodations office, but Mr. Rao would not give him the package. "No," he replied, "Swami said 'for madam.'"

Robert, returned with me. Mr. Kutumba Rao handed me the package wrapped in newspaper, and said, "Open it." I sat on the chair and unwrapped the gift. Mr. Rao declared, "It is silk! You are so blessed madam because Sai rarely gives out silk." I couldn't help but notice the plain, dirty newspaper used to cover this precious gift. The outer wrapping certainly symbolizes our body which covers the real treasure, the Atma, that lies within our bodies. Baba has said, *"Today's newspaper, tomorrow's waste paper."* It's true of the body, as well.

The sari is elegant, and it was my first silk sari. I was so happy. It was white with fine gold thread embroidery on the border and in a design on the material. The white color is really appropriate for American weddings because it symbolizes purity. This sari was so similar in design, to the one I wore but His was the genuine article, not synthetic, like mine. He had touched my heart so deeply that I couldn't control the tears flowing down my cheeks.

It has, now, been several years since our marriage day. Since then, Baba told me in an interview that my ring is to give me energy. When I first came to Baba my physical body was weak. He has strengthened it through a silver ring and gold colored stone. The gem has no outward reflection, only inwardly. You can see the golden streams of sunlight converging at the center of the ring, going inward into my body.

Aren't our "egos" so silly? All I could see on that marriage day was the outer beauty of the rings...not the inner purpose. There is a lesson in every word and action of Sai Baba. He is my guru, the one who points the way, and it is my duty – as a pupil to study His lessons with the eye of a researcher, examining every detail under a microscope.

"Why has Swami taken the camera?" I asked myself. I then remembered what a camera meant to me. I have often said that God created a live camera in our head. The camera is recording everything we see, hear, speak, taste and smell, then these daily "picture shows" determine our behavior. Sai Baba had accepted our camera, and that meant to me He was being responsible for purifying my "live camera," the senses.

Our entire wedding was a message for us to go inward and receive God. "The Atmic Wedding!"

He performed the formal rites of the ceremony in the outer interview room, but in the inner room, He became a personal and intimate God. Even when Robert tried to give Him the garland of flowers, He said, "No, heart to heart, inside." During the ring ceremony He scolded Robert for touching my hand, "Don't touch." This marriage is not binding us physically to one another, but binding each of us spiritually to God, and we could support one another through that process, and in the future.

He promised us that we will have greater health, peace, and happiness after marriage. It didn't happen the instant we returned home. Then I remembered His example of the fan. When you switch off the electricity, the blades still rotate for a while. Sometime during the following years, my heart healed, the love deepened, the peace spread, and the happiness grew. My dream of a loving marriage relationship was coming true!

THE MIND

The mind causes rebirth to beings.
The mind causes release to beings.
The mind confers victory to beings
In the struggle to attain the four:
dharma (righteousness), artha (wealth),
kama (desire), moksha (liberation).
The mind confers mergence everlasting (yoga nishta).

DIVINE DISCOURSE

The mind wills, yearns, prompts, and insists on effort and action. This activity is called sankalpa. Sankalpas are like commands (sasanas). Everyone has to be aware of the variety of the actions induced by these promptings. The mind is host to fifty million thoughts that appear and vanish like clouds. Some pass silently, but many stay and stir the mind into activity. Both these types are referred to as sankalpas. Until they are well understood against their vast background, man cannot live happily and in peace. How the mind functions and how it issues commands should be well understood by man; only then will he be able to utilize the infinite energy within himself for good.

Good sankalpas can elicit the best from man and help him to use all his energy for his improvement. Just like a fish which must swim against the current in order to survive, man must recognize bad sankalpas or urges as soon as they arise and render them ineffective by the systematic cultivation of beneficial sankalpas. In this way, he can save himself from troubles in life and live in peace.

Ships at sea are held on their desired course with the use of a compass. Without it, they risk being wrecked on the rocks or icebergs. Similarly, man has to navigate safely across the ocean of samsara (worldly life), with a calm, steady, one-pointed mind to guide him. Without such a mind, he will run into problems.

Man's face is an index, a reflection, a photograph of the mind with all of its moods, its decisions, its desires, its sankalpas. Every thought which comes into the mind is reflected on the face. The mind can be compared to a phonograph record. The words, songs, and sounds recorded therein can only be heard; they cannot be seen. On the contrary, the sankalpas of the mind cannot be heard, but can be seen as reflections on the face. Sankalpas (thoughts) which emanate from the mind are of two types: bad thoughts and good thoughts. Bad thoughts, such as anger, hatred, envy, despair, and pride, are reflected as ugliness on the face. Good thoughts, such as truth (sathya), love (prema), patience (sahanamu), compassion (karuna), kindness (daya), and empathy (sanubhuti), are reflected on the face as radiance and supreme peace.

The face is like a mold of the mind. Every single sankalpa (thought accepted and acted upon) is reflected on the face as a streak or line. The mind can be compared to a bulletin board which announces to all concerned the activities going on inside. Everything that happens inside the mind is also reflected on the face. Some people try to hide these reflections, but that is impossible. All attempts in this direction are as foolish as the ostrich's behavior when pursued. It buries its face in the loose sand and considers itself safe, even though its huge body can easily be seen. It is soon destroyed by hunters and dragged away. People who try to hide their sankalpas fail as miserably as the ostrich.

Every sankalpa has six characteristics: form, name, weight, color, size, and force. Sankalpas are not like mere letters written with black ink on a white sheet of paper. They undergo various changes, depending upon time and circumstance. Sankalpas breed further sankalpas. Mind is the root cause of the tree of sankalpas with its multiple branches, leaves, and fruits.

Sankalpas are projected through the eyes. There is a special connection between eyes and mind. Normally, we think that we are able to see things because of the eyes; but, in reality, eyes are not seeing things. It is because of the connection with the mind that the eyes are able to see. Similarly, ears are able to hear only when they come in contact with the mind.

Mind is the basis, the instrument of, and cause of all sense organs. It is their contact with the mind which enables the sense organs to perform their respective functions. One example: In ancient times, in order to protect the queen from being seen by the public, the queen's palace was built without any windows. Only small holes were left in the wall so that the queen, her companions, and her servants could see the outside world. The mind is like the queen *residing in the palace. The mind gets a view of the world, but the world cannot see the mind. Only the king and companions of the queen can see the queen inside the palace. Who can see the mind? Only the king of the sankalpas, the Knower (Aham), and the servants, sankalpas, can see the mind.*

The mind is formed by thoughts. The mind is a bundle of thoughts. These thoughts come from the ego, and ego comes from the Atma (indwelling Divinity). Atma-Ego-Mind: these three are closely related to each other. Sankalpas or inner resolutions with the same or similar qualities are attracted to one another like birds of a feather flock together. Cranes fly together as a flock, and they do not mix with crows; crows form their own groups. Among beasts of the forest, bison have herds of their own kind; these have no comradeship with elephants, which keep bison away and mingle only with elephants. Deer, too, form groups by themselves. Similarly, a musician moves around with other musicians. Teachers seek teachers for company. The reason for this is the similarities in their thinking.

Every decision the mind makes, whether to commit a thought to memory, to act upon it, or to reject it altogether, has a tremendous impact on the individual, for creation and all its contents can be described as the consequence of sankalpas. The eye is only a small opening, but it is capable of seeing the vast world. The eyes get the vision of the world because of their connection with the mind. Even if your eyes are open, if your mind is far away, you cannot see. So it is not the eyes that see and not the ears that hear-the mind does it all. Only when you inquire with an inner view, will you realize that the Atman is motivating the sense organs to function under the direction of sankalpas, or thoughts.

The results you experience depend upon your sankalpas. The sankalpa bears fruit which conforms to the seed from which it springs. To harvest good fruit, cultivate good sankalpas. You can easily indulge in bad sankalpas about others, but remember that you have to bear the consequences of such evil thought. Nobody can escape the fruits of sankalpas, good or bad. For example, one might entertain a desire to harm or injure someone else, and it might fructify as harm or injury to that other person. But it is certain that the sankalpa will rebound on the person who first welcomed it into his mind, bringing with it a hundredfold more harm and injury. A bad sankalpa hurts both the sender and his target. It is vitally important for you to realize this important fact about thoughts.

A poisonous worm can give only poison to all persons who handle it; you cannot expect amrit (sweet nectar) from it. Similarly, evil sankalpas have bad consequences, and nobody can escape from the suffering caused by them. That is the natural sequence of events. The epic Mahabharatha relates how the Kauravas fed and fostered their sankalpas to adopt various tactics to disgrace and eliminate their cousins, the Pandavas. Even though they succeeded in hurting the Pandavas to a certain extent, in return, the Kauravas were afflicted even more severely; the result was their total elimination, along with those who supported them. The Pandavas survived, crowned with glory. Good sankalpas help us and also help others.

Therefore, as soon as a thought sprouts in the mind as an urge or desire, one has to examine it with care to discover whether it is good or bad. Will it tarnish or promote one's reputation, hinder or help one's progress, weaken or strengthen one's character? If it is not going to be beneficial, cast it away from you as you would a foul, stinking object and save yourself by saturating your mind with good intentions.

How can you get rid of bad thoughts? Only through satsang (keeping good company). If you are in the midst of a foul odor, you have to light incense to get rid of it. Similarly, by developing good thoughts, you can ward off bad thoughts. When a thought arises, inquire about the impact of such a thought on your future.

Sometimes the nature of the sankalpa that motivates a person can be sensed by others. In ancient times, rishis (sages) were able to detect such sankalpas. Living together, they helped each other attain Self-realization (liberation).

A certain lone farmer in Holland illustrates this quite well. He left his brother and mother in order to live in peace and freedom, and settled on a forty-acre farm in a cottage he built thereon. He had an interest in poultry farming, and raised chickens. One night a fox came and ate some of the chickens. Its visits continued night after night, so the farmer made a decision (sankalpa) to kill the fox, and he stayed awake with a gun. Many nights passed, and he was unable to catch the fox. His chickens were disappearing. He could hear the flutter of the chickens as the fox approached, but he could not spot where it was. His vain vigil persisted for five long years. He consulted many elders about the mystery. A pure-hearted sympathizer told him, "Your mind is so free from blemish that even a tiny blot is patent to all. The fox is aware of your intention, and is taking clever measures to avoid being noticed." Animals have this capacity. It is a gift of nature. For example, a dog curled on the shoulder of the road will not be afraid of your approach when your sankalpas are good. On the other hand, if you pass by with bad sankalpas, planning to hit it, while even twenty feet away, the dog will rise and run. Even dogs have the power to sense good and bad sankalpas that arise in the mind. When animals have this sensitivity, why not men?

Man's sankalpas can be easily detected. If you look at the face of a person who has committed wrong, committed theft, scandalized another, or uttered a lie, you will notice the signs of confusion and fear. The anxiety makes the nerves weak and damages blood cells; the face becomes pale and lips quiver. The person's health is spoiled. If you hide the bad thoughts, you will suffer ill health. If you express bad thoughts, it will bring you shame. This is the effect of evil sankalpas. So the moment a bad thought comes, it must be plucked out by the roots, for all the unrest, crime, and anarchy in the world today is due to evil sankalpas.

Don't listen to bad words. Don't look at bad things. Don't speak evil of others. Don't perform bad deeds. You must see good, be good, do good, and hear good, so that evil intentions do not arise.

People who deal with criminals, such as lawyers, or read and write about them, such as journalists, are likely to be infected with evil thoughts, and their faces may be quite pale. Sadhakas (spiritual aspirants), who move in the company of the godly, are prone to develop serenity and compassion. Their faces will be filled with radiance, and you will be attracted to them. The face is the mirror of the mind, so try to purify your mind.

Light travels faster than sound, and the mind travels faster than light. Just as one needs good brakes to control a car going full speed, so, too, one has to exercise control over the mind; only then will you attain peace and happiness. Obey the mind's capricious notions, and you become a beast. Let discrimination control the vagaries of the mind, and you become a candidate for Divinity. Every urge must undergo a test, must be cleared by a judge, namely, the intellect (buddhi). If a thought prompts you to ridicule or defame another, dismiss it as unworthy.

The fruit of action comes from the seeds of sankalpas. From seeds of actions, you get the fruit of sadhana (spiritual discipline). From seeds of sadhana, you get the fruit of virtuous character. From seeds of virtuous character, you get the fruit of good fortune. So, if you want good fortune, you should have virtuous character. To obtain virtuous character, your sadhana must be good. Sadhana means the way you conduct yourself in day-to-day life. For good sadhana, your actions must be pure. In order to have pure actions, your thoughts must be pure. So, whether our fortune will be bad or good depends upon our sankalpas or thoughts. Whether we experience sorrow or joy, suffering or loss, pain or pleasure, all depends on our sankalpas.

If you want to cultivate good sankalpas, you must keep

good company. You cannot obtain good thoughts through education, wealth, health, fame, or power. You cannot gain them from without; they have to grow from within, from the heart, free from the weeds of pride and greed. If you feel that you are a wealthy person, a strong person, or a scholar, those thoughts will boost your ego. God has not given you education, wealth, strength, power, and wisdom to build your ego. God has given these virtues to you so that you will experience joy and share that joy with others. With intelligence, develop goodness; with education, enhance your discrimination; with discrimination, develop humility. These result from good sankalpas.

This is the lesson people have to learn today. Cultivate sath sankalpas (good thoughts) by seeking out and abiding in satsang (good company). Planting poisonous seeds, people hope to get delicious fruits. Why blame God when bitter seeds do not yield sweet fruit? It is you who cultivated them. Therefore, sow good seeds and reap good fruit. There are fifty million sankalpas. Understand the tremendous impact of these thoughts; then you will be able to recognize the sacredness of human birth.

Man is the only animal which imbibes and expresses Ananda (bliss). No other animal has this quality. So why is man unhappy? Our actions are opposed to the nature of man, so we are in misery. The smile on the face is the blooming of the joy that fills the heart. It wafts away discontent and depression from other faces. When you smile, you should not produce sound, nor show your back teeth. Develop thoughts which will lead you to good actions so that you can smile and make others smile. You can do this only through spirituality (sadhana).

These are the four antakaranas:

manas - mind

buddhi - intellect

chitta - heart

ahamkara - ego (the limited I-sense)

The first one is the mind (manas). If you control your mind, you will have fulfillment of life. Mind is responsible for rebirth, and mind can also release you from the need to be born again. Through the mind, you can obtain righteousness, wealth, fulfillment of desires, and liberation. Through the mind karmayoga (the path of action), jnanayoga (the path of wisdom), bhaktiyoga (the path of devotion), and rajayoga (the path of meditation), you can reach culmination. The mind can be an instrument to gain success on any of these paths in the struggle to gain the goal of life.

Mind is responsible for both bondage and liberation. The source of human life is the mind. Everything in the world emerges from the mind. Everything in the world is created by the mind. Fill your mind with good thoughts. Hold it steadily on the right path so that it can merge into the Source from whence it came. Merge the mind in Aham or I; then the limited I-sense becomes I, your true God-self, or unlimited identity. If you keep the mind separate from its Source, you identify yourself as a limited man, an ego. When you say, "I am I" (Aham Aham), you declare yourself to be unlimited, infinite.

I am man = ahamkara (ego, the thinker)

I am I = Aham (the Knower)

If you add akara (form) to Aham, it becomes ahamkara. So, as long as you have form (body consciousness), you have ahamkara. Merge in Aham, Divinity, and become I (Brahman), the perpetual consciousness of God.

In the Sanskrit language, the first letter of the alphabet is "A" and the last one is "Ha." When you combine A and Ha, it becomes Aha. If you combine these, life becomes sanctified; then Aham should be transformed to Atmatatwa (knowledge of the Atman). Aham Atma has three names:

Aham dehasmi = I am this body (gross body)

Aham jeevasmi = I am the jiva (soul, subtle body)

Aham Brahmasmi = I am God (causal body)

In order to achieve the mergence, the consummation, saturate the mind with sath sankalpas. Remember: "From good thoughts, obtain a good mind; from a good mind, obtain God."

- SATHYA SAI BABA

PARENTS

**START THE DAY WITH PRAYER
FILL THE DAY WITH PRACTICE
END THE DAY WITH PATIENCE
THIS IS THE WAY TO PARENT**

I never realized, as a new parent, that it took a special psychology, philosophy, or theology to raise a child. They just naturally grew up, I thought. My only teachers on parenting were my own parents. If I followed their rules, then I assumed my children would develop as I did. That couldn't have been further from the truth. My concept never allowed for the additional factor of change. How was I to know that our world was to change so drastically from my childhood days? I hadn't noticed it happening!

As a child, I lived in a small suburb in St. Louis County. My family, grandparents, and relatives all lived in the same neighborhood. Everyone knew their neighbors. All the children of my parents' friends were my childhood schoolmates. Our life was centered around the Catholic Church, one block away.

I attended daily mass before school. All of my outside activities or entertainment were centered around my family, church, and school. I loved to play sports, so most of my free time was spent with our coach, a Catholic priest who taught us basketball in the winter months and softball in the summer.

My father's family was gifted in music and all of us were very much encouraged by Grandma. I loved to play the piano and would spend hours practicing. Three of my father's sisters were nuns, and one of them taught me music at the church convent.

Our family lifestyle followed a pattern, a daily routine. Monday, Mom and Grandma did the washing; Tuesday, the ironing; Wednesday the baking – my favorite day. My parents and grandmother who lived with us, provided a stable secure atmosphere for a child.

Family tradition also played a major role in my life, especially during holidays. On Christmas Eve, the entire family – all the grandparents, aunts, and uncles and my many cousins – gathered at my uncle's home for Christmas cheer. We sang Christmas carols around the piano, exchanging gifts from godparents, drinking fruit punch and eating Christmas treats. Without fail, when the clock struck 11:00 p.m., we all left to attend the Midnight Mass. Every year, Christmas, Easter, Thanksgiving, etc. was spent with our family in the same manner. As a child, it gave me a feeling of belonging and a cherished event to look forward to.

My early years were influenced by my parent's norms, which happened to be the same as all our relatives, friends and neighbors. My playmates were raised with the same values as mine. Many of these values were laid down by our religion. My parents had a secure support system for raising their children. They acknowledged their responsibility for their children and lived the teachings of Jesus to the best of their ability. There were no conflicting beliefs to disturb or challenge their principles. They were good people.

Television entered our household when I was in high school. We were awed by the lighted screen that took us to places and things we had never seen. Friends and neighbors all gathered around the new set in the neighborhood. How quickly it became a habit. After dinner we would hurry and wash the dishes and sit in front of the screen. We didn't want to miss a thing. Dad could take us to the show without wearing a shirt and tie and never leaving his favorite easy chair. It was all too convenient.

We were fascinated by the magical evening entertainment. The programs then were wholesome and were suited for family viewing. We laughed at the talent shows and comedians. They reminded my dad of the vaudeville shows at the theater, how he would laugh!

How were we to know that this innocent screen would also bring into our homes the war of Vietnam, the crime and violence of our streets, the assassination of our President, movies with sex, divorce, drugs and child abuse, etc.?

Television had very little influence on my development,

but it would play a major role in my children's development.   My generation was the first to raise children who lived with the influence of daily television. It had invaded the privacy of our homes.

If I were to point out the single object that created the most unwanted values in my home, I would have to say with absolute conviction, the television set. Yes, it can be used for educational and inspirational shows but these are   limited   and when they are offered the children are not interested and would much prefer the shows that their peers watch.   This invention created desires in my children and gave them values that differed from ours. The instrument that baby-sat for us when the children were young caused arguments and conflicts in their teen-age years because they were learning different values. The good fairy had turned into an ogre!

If I were asked to name one thing that parents could do to ease the job of parenting......I would reply without a moments hesitation remove the television or censor the programs using Sai Vision instead of Television.

The influence of television that freed my time with the children   when young, consumed my time when they were   older, because   I   had to defend and communicate Sai values that were different to the mores of society as shown on the television.

Sai Baba says, *"You must bear in mind that the years of youth are the most precious years in one's life, and they should not be wasted or misspent. To let children watch television from 6.p.m. to 10 p.m. is to make them forget all   that   they   have learned at school or college.   In* *addition, they learn many evil things. If television is used for teaching good things, it can serve a worthy purpose. But that is **not** the case. The younger generation is being ruined by undesirable films and television programs. Their minds are being poisoned. It is not a sign of parental love to let children be ruined in this manner. Even parents should avoid going to cinemas. All the crimes and violence we witness today are largely the result of the evil influence of films on young minds."*

We have allowed mass entertainment to become subliminal violent programming, and most often we are not aware of the harm. Through the images impressed on us by others with different values to us we are misguided and misled.

Not only did we have the new influence of worldwide television, but also we lived in an age of increasing mobility. There were many families who like us were transferred with their jobs and lost the support of the extended family.

My generation also had a "values earthquake" that examined, challenged, and threatened all the mores of our culture. The revolution of the Sixties questioned our educational systems, government spending, foreign involvement, our material lifestyle, our patriotism, our sexual morality, the role of women, our marriage system and even our church. The Catholic church had its own shake-up. It turned the altar around, dropped the Latin, and opened the doors, and tried to shed new light on an outdated interpretation of old spiritual laws and beliefs. This Ecumenical movement attempted to reach out and recognize other Christian doctrines as having validity.

Meanwhile, I became a mother relying on the parenting skills I learned by example from my mom and dad. Their methods of raising children in a controlled environment were not working for me. My generation were pioneers, blazing an unfamiliar trail. We did not know the consequences of this new expanded age of information. There seemed to be no current role model of parenting to follow. How many times I would say, "I wonder what Mom and Dad would have done in this circumstance?" Change and mobility replaced ages of routine and tradition. I became a parental victim, caught with my children, in the swell of this new wave of exceptional change.

Parenting became a smorgasbord of recommendations from 'experts'. I'd try a little of this and a little of that. I was continually groping for a solution. We used discipline; then we were told that discipline didn't allow the child freedom of expression to develop creativity. We let the little darlings express themselves, and what chaos! It's not that discipline or creative expression are wrong, I just allowed them to the extreme. Creative expression or freedom of expression used in the boundaries of discipline is excellent.

In the Fifties, popular psychology publicized the concept that parents were responsible for most of their children's behavior, good and bad. It was no longer possible to blame Uncle Harry's idiosyncrasies for little John's temper tantrum, or attribute little Mary's showing off to Aunt Irene's role model. No, now every time my children misbehaved, it was Robert's or my fault. We conscientiously but not fully consciously took on this enormous burden and an overload of guilt that remained in our consciousness long after the concept was eventually shown to be only partly true.

I tried in every way to improve my success as a parent, but our children kept slipping away from our influence. Daily, we would be faced with unfamiliar childhood behavior like disrespect to parents and, frankly, we did not know how to stop it. There was so much information and change taking place, we could find no way of applying the brakes, or to digest, understand and test the consequences of our new lifestyle. My own moral values were in constant conflict with current morality. I felt my children were being victimized and influenced by society, and our arms were never long enough to protect them.

The job of parenting today is awesome, and parents have my greatest love and empathy. But perhaps you dear reader, can learn from the teachings of Sai Baba and our experience. How I wish that I had known Swami's teachings to help guide me, when my children were growing up. I continually wondered whether I was too lenient or too strict. I was inconsistent with discipline, sometimes I followed through with our house rules and sometimes I was just too tired to fight to control the children. Children have a way of pestering you until you give in to their every wish.

Since then Swami has taught me that children need stability, consistency, discipline, routine and tradition in their lives to balance the disruptive forces of change that are prevalent in society today, and the changes in themselves as they are growing up. With Sai's code of conduct we can remain firm and consistent because it is Truth.

Every lesson that Sai teaches us is based on self-application. He insists that we always be an example. He tells us if we speak about His Divinity and people are not ready to listen, we are blowing our breath in the wind. I thought, "Boy! that sounds like my kids when I'm talking to them. The more I talk; the more they tuned me out." So I took Sai's advice and tried to reach my children through example.

He said, *"My Life Is My Message"* and doesn't that say it all? Becoming a good example of Sai Baba's teachings is no easy job. I remember when I first became a devotee. I was overwhelmed with the amount of habits I wanted to change. The more books I read, the more faults I'd find in myself to correct. I nearly slipped into feeling sorry for myself and found an excuse to forget the whole idea. Swami knows that we're not perfect, so I could not hide behind past guilt or future failure to prevent present action. The key He tells us is to **"START"**. I knew the greatest gift I could give my family was to apply His teachings, change my behavior and perhaps some day they might be able to feel and see His Love through me.

Sai says, *"Parents must correct themselves before they try to correct their children."* He tells us that the parent is the first and the most significant teacher for the pre-school child. I can remember that my babies would easily respond to my mood. If I was happy and peaceful, most of the time so were they. But if I was stressful or aggravated in any way, they felt it and became cranky.

"Children are charming saplings, full of promise, who can be made, by wise care and well-directed love, to blossom into ideal citizens, able to understand, appreciate, and practice the tough discipline laid down in the ancient wisdom for attaining self-knowledge and knowledge of the Universe, which is only another aspect of the Self. The earlier years of life are the most crucial, and so the mother and father have to share the responsibility for the proper upbringing. The skills, the attitude, the prejudices, and the emotions that make or mar the future are all built into the foundation of character during those crucial years. The parents must lay the foundation strong and straight. But what equipment have the parents now for this task? They have no deep knowledge of their own culture; they have no faith in its values; they practice no spiritual discipline; they have no mental peace. Children must grow up in the atmosphere of reverence, devotion, mutual service and cooperation. They must be taught respect for parents, teachers and elders"...... "Parents first, teachers next, playmates and companions later, then the leaders who command the allegiance of millions. These Leaders should all be constantly examining themselves, whether they are fit examples to be followed by the children of the land. These shape the character and so shape the future of the country."*

As a new mother, I was not very aware of children and I guess this is why an incident with my first child, Carol, made a lasting impression on me.

One day, I broke a treasured vase. I was angry, threw it in the waste basket and cursed. Several days later Robert's mom came for a visit. We took Carol, then one-and-a half years old for a walk. She fell and repeated the exact cuss word she heard from me a few days before. Not only did she use the exact word, she imitated my behavior precisely!

The old adage, "Don't do as I do, do as I tell you" did not work for me. When we slipped and did what we told the children not to do, they were the first to tell us. When you have children they are a constant mirror reflection, and when they get older and smarter they are talking mirrors. Sai says, *"Parents must correct themselves before they try to correct their children."*

"If we sow a thought today, we reap an act tomorrow. If we sow an act today, we reap a habit tomorrow. If we sow a habit today, we reap a character tomorrow. If we sow a character today we reap a destiny tomorrow."

Sai Baba is constantly teaching us. In one of our interviews He told Robert that he is a good man, and He told me that I have a sweet heart. After that interview, I would catch myself while observing my behavior, and think Swami says I have a sweet heart, so I must show it and be sweet. I tried even harder to live up to His words.

I became more conscious of what messages I was delivering and how I was programming my children. I felt none of them had a really good self-image as all of them could have more self-confidence. I wanted them to feel as good about themselves as Swami made me feel about myself. He says, *"Self-confidence leads to self-*

satisfaction, self-satisfaction leads to self-sacrifice and self-sacrifice leads to self-realization.''

I wondered if it would work for them as it did for me. They already had some self-confidence but since there are varying degrees of goodness and sweetness there is always room for improvement. Sai tells us that *"Parents have the primary responsibility to mold the character of their children.''* But, today, with the outside world invading the privacy of my home and influencing my children, I was no longer the only primary influence. How do I take responsibility for the whole world coming into my living room during the evening news? I felt like I had lost control of my home environment and I didn't know how to get it back. But I was beginning to understand that if I was to be responsible for their behavior then I had to be responsible for setting more control factors.

"Parents today tend to lavish too much affection on their children. But such affection alone is not enough. There should also be control over the children. There should be both 'love' and 'law'. Only when both love and restraint are present will the love prove beneficial.

"It is not wrong to love children. But you parents should learn how to love them. Whenever the children go astray wittingly or unwittingly, parents should hasten to correct their faults and bring them to the right path. The obligations of parents does not end with providing food, schooling, and knowledge of worldly matters. The children should also be provided with right values. They should not be made to think that the acquisition of

wealth is the be-all and end-all of life."

Since I met Sai Baba, I have had to rethink and reorientate my parenting skills. Swami says, we lavish too much affection on our children, and not enough control.

My parents provided a better lifestyle for me, than they had known and I desired to do this for my children. But somewhere in my eagerness, I lost the balance of love and law. I stretched the term "giving love" to mean giving the children almost anything they wanted, including permitting unacceptable behavior. Providing a better lifestyle, better home, clothes, toys, and food had expanded into a lifestyle full of unhappiness.

I not only wanted to spare my children physical discomfort but psychological discomfort as well. I had given myself an impossible and unreasonable goal to achieve. I was not able to fulfill all their desires and yet I felt obligated to do so.

Sai tells us, *"Joy is a brief interlude between two sorrows."* Then "Why am I trying to remove all their sorrow...even sorrow in the form of discipline?" I asked myself.

Many times I have observed Sai Baba act as my mother and father. Symbolically mother represents love and father represents discipline. If my behavior needs to be corrected, Swami will go to great lengths to accomplish this. But Sai Baba is not interested in a short term goal, of making me happy only in the present, but He is preparing me for the long term goal of merging with God, Eternal Bliss.

I again asked myself, how do I relate this to my relationship with my children? Am I too interested in having my children's short term approval? What happens when they are confronted as adults with disappointments and the problems we must face in life? What will they think of me then, when they are not prepared to cope?

If I give my children too much love without discipline, they become spoiled. If I give my children too much discipline without love they become rebellious. Again the need for greater balance. I decided to take more control where I could in my home, by enforcing consistent house rules.

Since Sai Baba uses both parents, mother's love and father's discipline, I learned that not one parent only is needed to administer love and discipline but both need to take an active part. Parenting today is far more stressful than when I was young, and because of the greater distractions the children need even more supervision. The job can overwhelm a single parent. Together, Robert and I committed ourselves to share the duty. We also decided that we would take one house rule per month, and practice enforcing it with consistency and love. We also decided that every decision concerning the kids would be made jointly, because they loved to play one of us off against the other. This way we represented a united front.

Sai tells us that there are bumps and jumps. When we struggle with a problem whatever it may be, we grow more. We jump ahead instead of taking one step. This struggle develops inner strength, builds more character, increases our awareness of others and instills a desire to give.

The very thing that I was trying to develop in my children was inner character and a good self-image. I was destroying with over-indulgence. I was always giving to them but it was rare that they thought of us. They were self-centered, "the ME generation." My children were no different than their Mom. I've learned through adversity. So why was I trying to remove most of their struggles? For example: Why was it so hard for them to give respect to God, parents, teachers, and others. And what about giving silence instead of back talk? When asked to do chores, was it essential to constantly repeat the request until it was forceful enough for them to do the task? And how about giving patience and care to brothers and sisters instead of fighting and criticizing?

Sai Baba says, *"love is only expressed through giving."* If I do most of the giving, how can my children learn the art of loving by giving to others. A good self-image is created by inner achievement as well as outside achievement. I had recognized their sports, music and scholastic abilities far more than their inner achievement. And in all fairness, there had been more to recognize outwardly.

If my children were not being constantly entertained .... they were **bored.** And believe it or not, my grandchildren are even worse. We have amused these children with videos, computer games, show-biz pizza parties, dancing, swimming, karate and art lessons. Then there's sports. They have football, softball, baseball teams, golf, tennis, movies, shopping and eating out. Have I left anything out? I ask you, how can they be bored?

"Discipline trains you to put up with disappointments; you will know that the path of life has both ups and downs, that every rose has its thorn. Now, people want roses without thorns. Life has to be one saga of sensual pleasure, a picnic all the time. When this does not happen, you turn wild and start blaming others. If each one cares for his own pleasures, how can society progress? How can the weak survive? Mine, not thine–this sense of greed is the root of all evil. This distinction is applied even to God...My God, not yours! Your God, not mine!"

Swami's rules of right conduct seemed so far removed from the norms of our culture. As I told His teachings to the children, my voice seemed like a whisper compared to the stereo amplifiers of the present generation. I wondered if my children ever heard a word or noticed our example?

Parents who know Sai Baba have a bonfire of hope burning at Prashanti Nilayam. Because He concentrates most of His time and energy on children and the education of children. His teachings are helpful, clear and concise. The main existing problem is our ability to weaken His teachings by inconsistency, self-interpretation, and failure to practice. But for any small effort that we make He magnifies the benefits with His Divine grace.

Swami has many students in His schools. One day I came across the following teachings which govern the conduct in His schools.

"I insist on discipline. *Man has in him certain specific attributes which have to be developed and fostered so that he can rise up to his full stature. If these are ignored or allowed to lie fallow, he exists on the animal level only. Discipline alone can make him grow into his heritage. Children's minds are innocent, tender, and pure. The snake gourd is apt to grow crooked if left alone, so gardeners tie a stone to its end and the weight pulls it straight as it grows longer and longer. The minds of children and of youth are also apt to grow crooked under the influence of the sensuous films, the hollow hypocritical atmosphere created by the elders, the lure of glitter and glamour and of a false sense of adventure and fame. So parents and schools have to attach the stone of discipline and make them grow straight and true.*

"The stone should not be too heavy, lest it snap the gourd in two! Avoid extremes, at all times, in all cases. Disciplinary rules have to be well thought out and adapted to the age group they wish to correct. The atmosphere must be so charged, that obedience to discipline comes automatically with a full heart.

"I insist on reverent obedience to parents. *The mother who bore you, the father who nurtured you, and the teacher who opened your eye to the mystery of nature in and around you all have to be revered. However high you may rise in social status, however huge may be your bank account, if your parents are neglected in distress,* *your life has been a tragic waste. The parents gave you this body and fostered the intelligence and love that are embedded in it, so gratitude is their due. If you do not honor the parents who are the creators in human form, how can you learn to honor the Creator in the Divine? Moreover, the parents reveal to you the glory of God and the means of worshipping Him; they are the first representatives of the authority which you meet with, and you will learn through them, how to submit to the Lord. As the twig is bent, so the tree is inclined.*

"**I insist on regulated food and play.** *Regulate the food habits of the children; food determines to a large extent health and intelligence, emotions, and impulses. Set limits on the quality and quantity of food, as well as to the number of times it is consumed and the timings. Recreation too, has to be moral and elevating and in the company of the righteous and God-fearing.*

"**I insist on rigorous allocation of time for study,** *singing spiritual songs, meditation, etc. Bhajan has to start in childhood and has to continue. It must be the constant companion of man, his solace and strength. Do not postpone it to old age, for it is the essential food for the mind. Tell your children stories from the Scriptures of all religions so they can realize that the saints and seers of all lands are equally good and great. Let the children realize that prayer is universal and that prayer in any language addressed to any Name reaches the same God. Do not keep the young ones idle and unoccupied. Every second is a precious gift. Time well used is like food well digested. It sustains and strengthens the students.*

"I also recommend some items of service, *like nursing the sick. Visit patients in the hospitals, read nice storybooks sitting by the side of the patients in the beds, write letters for them, and generally be kind and friendly to them in their loneliness and pain. Go to the slum area, move like lighted lamps full of love and sympathy, and help the people there get things done which will improve their health, add to their income, and advance their education.*

"I condemn *frivolous talk, luxurious living, deleterious habits, addiction to films, horror-comics, pen-friends, exotic dress, outlandish coiffures designed to draw attention to oneself, etc. By these means, boys and girls are slowly drawn into non-righteous and immoral ways."*

I have heard it said, that movies and television of sex, horror and violence have no influence over our children's behavior. Yet, businesses spend millions of dollars on commercials because what we hear and what we see do influence us to purchase their products. How can it affect our buying habits, but not our moral habits? Such an argument is not only illogical but patently untrue.

"Avoid films, for though they may be advertised as very educative and inspiring, the producers, in their greed for profits, smuggle in low, vulgar debasing scenes in order to please raw, untrained minds. Don't allow the virus of vice to infect your brains. If that happens, you descend to levels worse than the beasts."

My children liked to go to movies with their friends.. This has been an acceptable form of entertainment for children since the nineteen thirties, when talking movies became world-wide. But many of the films were not acceptable. The film industry was exploiting the animal nature of man, in the name of entertainment and relaxation.

I would get pressured by my children to attend the movies with their friends on weekends. It was a social outing for them. Our problem was to find a decent movie for them to attend. They would plead with me, "Please mom, my friends' parents said he can go. If they think it's all-right, why don't you?" "Mother, you're so old-fashioned," they would say. I replied, "If old-fashioned means I want nothing to harm you, then you're right, I'm old-fashioned."

In some cases, I did not review the movie the children were going to see. Instead, I relied on the judgment of my friends who had seen it, as we rarely went ourselves. I soon found out that didn't work, because their standard for judging movies differed from Sai Baba's and mine. Parents have asked me, "What about the times that I have no control over my child's viewing?" This happens especially with television when the child is older.

I remember Sai Baba's example. He knows we are going to slip and make mistakes along the journey of life. Knowing this doesn't stop Him from telling us what's correct, and when we do fail, we hear His voice within again repeating the same axiom.

"Parents should not allow children to fall away from their control and wander about without compass or anchor. Many parents feed and fondle their children and then, in the name of freedom, leave them to find their own friends

and pleasures. They take them to films regardless of the impressions they create on their tender minds. They entertain the friends of their children but do not inquire their antecedents or habits."

I really didn't like to tell my children, NO. It's much easier to say yes, then there is no conflict. Somehow our 'permissive' society has reached a stage were any restriction that is imposed is interpreted as a demonstration of dislike or lack of love. So the children triggered inner conflict in me. I wanted them to know how much I loved them and yet they so easily interpreted my caring restrictions as a lack of love.

I have observed Sai Baba who is total love, respond to my requests. He certainly tells me 'no' if it is something that would be harmful to me. His love is so strong, so universal, and so easy to feel that I learned to rely on His wisdom; and hoped that my children would rely on mine.

For example, when I want an interview and He doesn't give it. Although I have cried, begged, pleaded and/or promised, He complies with my request in His time not mine. I learned from Him to say "No" with more ease and to say it with love and firmness. Somehow experiencing His example helped me to become stronger. If I weaken to the pressure of my children and say "Yes" when it should be "No" how will they ever learn to be firm and to say NO when it is necessary? I am their role model.

Peer pressure can force a good child to remain silent

and follow the crowd. That's every parents nightmare! I wanted my children to learn to say "NO" with dignity and self-confidence, (like Baba,) and not be pressured into drugs, drinking, or promiscuous sex or any other behavior that was ethically dubious, immoral or harmful.

Sai says, *"It's not the standard of living that's important, it's the manner of living."*

Sri Sathya Sai Baba is very clear concerning the manner in which we are to rear our children. He asks us to be strict, disciplined, and obedient as parents and children. The following statement He makes I found to be very strong, clear and helpful.

"It is the duty of parents to set children on the right path from their early years. They should not hesitate to correct them and even punish them when the children take to wrong ways. The best way they can show their love for their children is to do everything necessary to make them follow the right path. If any teenager proves intractable or incorrigible, they should not hesitate to disown him. It is better to have one good son rather than a brood of bad children."

Some of my children wanted freedom of selection, to choose for themselves. They waited impatiently for when they could be on their own. This so-called freedom is a myth. We are never free of our Atma, which speaks to us through our conscience.

Baba says, *"People in the West talk about freedom. What is this freedom? Does it mean acting as you please, doing what you like? Not at all. True freedom consists in keeping the senses under control, - otherwise one is simply a slave to the senses."*

We give the individual person the freedom to smoke, drive while intoxicated, to read pornographic material, etc. But where in society is there the collective individual's freedom to breathe pure smokeless air, freedom to drive without fear of accidents due to drunken drivers, freedom to walk on the street without being molested, abused or mugged?

Sai says that 'freedom' does not mean any behavior is permissible. The fashionable narrow vision of freedom gives the individual person freedom to misuse and abuse others and does not give "we the people" a safer and healthier environment to live, work, and raise our children in. I want my children to understand that their actions will always affect the well being of someone or thing. They must understand that their behavior affects all the family, and we are never free to choose only for our own benefit; that is selfishness. We must learn to accept the consequences of our actions, use discrimination, select and support behavior that is beneficial to everyone. Freedom must be used for the "brotherhood of man" not just for the individual brother.

"There is a proper meaning to the word Dharma (Right Action). All those actions which do not come in the way of others, which do not impinge on the freedom of others, such can be described as Dharma. Here is a small example of this. You are holding a long stick and playing with it, moving it this way and that, and at the same time you are walking down a main street. This street is a busy public

thoroughfare. You say, "I have every right to move anywhere I want. This is my freedom. This is my Dharma." Well, if this is your Dharma, then the person who is coming in the opposite direction has every right to save himself from being hit by your stick. You are indulging in an activity which is likely to put other people walking on the street in danger. However, right conduct expects you to act so that you do not come in the way of other people walking on the same road. If you can conduct yourself in a way that does not cause any inconvenience and trouble to the freedom of others, then you are behaving according to Dharma."

I was taught that God gives you a gift when you are married. He gives the gift of life – a child. It is not our child, but His. We are the foster parents while this soul is on earth. I certainly would not want to return this child in a lesser state than when I received it. In fact I want to return each child to God in a more advanced spiritual state.

One of the most treasured gifts given to devotees from Sai Baba is the lingam. If I possessed a lingam, I would perform daily spiritual rituals with great devotion, and protect, love and care for this magnificent symbol of creation. Then I thought, we too have been given a lingam......a human lingam, in the form of a child. Now that my children are grown and in their twenties, I can see glimmers of hope. Some of the seeds that we planted so long ago are sprouting. Sometimes I even hear them repeat to their children the same axioms we taught them. (Don't be discouraged, dear readers.) All of us have more hope today than ever before with our

215

beloved Sai Baba here on earth.

I feel better now about myself as a parent because I can finally see some good strong results. As a parent, especially a mother, we can devote our entire life, day and night, helping our children, and it takes a long time for our work to mature. Its so easy to lose sight of this long-term goal, and want quick results. But we must remember that love is never wasted and hopefully someday it will fructify.

"Love is not saying – love is doing"

When Robert and I became devotees, the ages of my children were 19, 17, 12, and 10. They had been brought up in the Catholic faith, and we attended church every Sunday. As new followers of Baba, we placed His pictures in our home and worshiped Him as God. This confused our children, especially the younger two. How could I expect them to understand our concept of God, when most adults are not able? The children were targets of ridicule from their peers.

A year later, we attended the First Central Regional Conference in the U.S.A. where Dr. Hislop was a guest speaker. I consulted with him on this problem and his advice was most helpful. He told us to keep our pictures and prayer room private, and continue to educate our children in the religion they were taught, worshipping the form of Jesus Christ. We maintained their weekly religion class and Sunday Mass.

Dr. Hislop advised me that if we use any force on the children, trying to convince them that Sai is God, they will rebel and never be free to accept Sai as God. I was indeed familiar with the word rebellion, and nothing more needed to be said. We followed his advice, and it worked for us. Sai Baba tells us that He has not come to start a new religion. He says,

> *"There is only one Religion, the Religion of Love.*
> *There is only one Language, the Language of the Heart.*
> *There is only one Race, the Race of Humanity.*
> *There is only one God, and He is Omnipresent."*

We continued to learn and practice Sai's teachings, without preaching. When we referred to God, we never identified him in any form. We encouraged the children's relationship with Jesus. As the years passed, through practice, we were living some of Sai's teachings, and the older children could see the difference in our behavior. They could feel Sai's love through us. Even my mother observed our transformation and remarked, "I don't understand Sai Baba, but I've seen the change in you and Robert and whatever he's doing to you is good." Her remark pleased me immensely.

Hopefully our children are free to answer Sai's call, when it comes, because we did not block its reception by forcing them to become devotees. God will call each of them when it is their special time. Many parents want that time to be NOW; but have faith, relax, and be happy. Baba is responsible for their journey to Him. We are responsible for their love and devotion to God in any form.

Sai Baba has taught me that Truth prevails forever, its nature is unchanging. Truth can be identified because it does not change from age to age. Qualities of kindness, respect, honor to parents remain the same and don't change their meaning with each new generation, so they belong to Truth and express it. Now that I know this, my children or other people, can no longer convince me that I'm wrong. My conscience is steady and more consistent.

One of the most rigorous feats to accomplish is swimming against the current, and this is exactly what Sai is asking us parents to do. He is telling us to swim against the trendy current in our society, to set our children upon a course that will separate them from the present stream of values, or rather no true values. Realize that although a difficult task, our effort will bring down God's grace and turn the tide in our favor.

"Man is born in society; he is bred in society; he is shaped well or ill by the subtle influence of society. He in his turn, as a member of society, influences the people who contact him. His life is turned or twisted by the standards, modes, and behavior patterns of the society into which he is born through the effects of his accumulated actions. The body and the country are inextricably intertwined. The body is one encasement; the country is another for the spirit of man. Use society for your uplift; try to shape society so that it will help the uplift of individuals and not turn them away from God."

Years ago, one day when I was struggling with my parental duty and responsibility, Sai gave me the following thoughts:

PARENTS

Society says give the children what they want.
Sai-ety says teach the children not to want.

Society says wealth is material.
Sai-ety says wealth is Spiritual.

Society says educate to develop our market.
Sai-ety says educate to develop our character.

Society says Take.
Sai-ety says Give.

Society acknowledges youth and forgets the aged.
Sai-ety prepares youth to honor the aged.

Society encourages overuse and misuse.
Sai-ety encourages preserve and conserve.

Society says satisfy your senses.
Sai-ety   says satisfaction is from controlling your senses.

Society says don't give away your time, sell it.
Sai-ety says don't waste your time, volunteer it.

Society says dress to attract and excite.
Sai-ety says clean up and cover up.

Society says mothers have the right to a career.
Sai-ety says the only right career for mothers is to be one.

Society says exalt yourself.
Sai-ety says humble yourself.

Society abuses parents.
Sai-ety respects parents.

Society says there is no physical proof of God.
Sai-ety says **"IT IS THE PHYSICAL PROOF OF GOD!"**

"The Peace of the World depends on peace and amity between nations; the peace of a nation depends on the peace between the concomitant units the villages, the families, and finally, the individuals of each family.

219

So, every individual has a responsibility to love others, have faith in them, and revere them as sparks of the Divine. Every man has to cultivate the virtues of tolerance, forbearance and brotherliness.

"If one loses wealth, he may regain it by some ruse or other. If he loses health, some doctor might prescribe a tonic to win it back. If one loses status and authority, he may by sheer luck gain them back. If virtue is lost, it is lost forever; nothing can restore the pristine purity. So one has to be ever vigilant and never slacken.

"The greatest of the virtues is love. Love is the basis of character. You may have all other desirable things in plenty; but if you have no character, that is to say, virtue, which is threaded on a string of love, you can have no genuine peace. Money comes and goes! But, morality? It comes and grows! Morality has to be grown in the heart by feeding it with love, then only can we have justice, security, law, and order. If love declines among the people, nations will weaken and mankind will perish.

"If there is righteousness in the heart
There will be beauty in character;
If there is beauty in character
There will be harmony in the home.

"When there is harmony in the home,
There will be order in the nation.
When there is order in the nation,
There will be peace in the world."

INNER VOICE

We arose very early on April II, 1984, packed our gear, and joined our two lady passengers in the lobby of the Shilton Hotel Sundaram, presently a permanent resident staying at Swami's ashram who comes from the U.S., and Maggie, a lass from Australia, who came for a short term visit. Both had asked "if" Swami was travelling to Ooty could they join Robert and I in the taxi. So this morning we were leaving for Ooty and were very curious about the day's upcoming events.

It was exactly 6:00 a.m. when we asked our taxi driver to pull over underneath a large shade tree, outside the city of Bangalore, on the only road to Ooty. If Swami was travelling to Ooty He would have to pass this way. Of course, there was the possibility that He had travel with Him, the way would be clear. We were excited, had faith and were prepared to wait.

Our fourth trip to India had started five days earlier, when Bala Gopal, our friend, greeted us at the airport with his taxi. Gopal said that Baba was expected in Whitefield any day. Baba had been at Prashanti Nilayam for two months and was supposed to inspect the building progress of His new home being built at Brindavan. We were here last year when the old residence was torn down. We spent the night in Bangalore and had a good rest.

Since there was no news of Baba's departure from Prashanti, we left to go there at noon. Each time we traveled that road, we saw changes being made in the valley. The road had more paved surface, there was a greater abundance of agriculture, more newly planted trees, and cleaner villages. It clearly showed that if you continue on the road to Sai Baba, progress would follow.

We had scheduled our trip to arrive at Prashanti for evening darshan. As we entered the first gate, Gopal said "That looks like Swami's white Mercedes." We slowed down, and pulled over. The excitement of seeing Swami swelled in our hearts, as His car slowed down, pulled over, and turned around. We got out of our car to greet Him. He rolled down His car window and said "Go, I will be there shortly." What a wonderful way to start our trip, being greeted by our Lord, Himself. There was no evening darshan, and the kindness of Baba to stop on the road was savored in our hearts. Only He knew how much we longed to see Him. The following morning, Baba left for Bangalore.

About a month before we departed for India, I had asked my husband Robert if he could take two extra days off from work. I told him that I felt that Swami wanted us to come two days earlier than planned. Robert checked with his boss and changed our air tickets. Now we knew the reason. It was the only time Baba was in Prashanti during our month's stay, and we brought some supplies to give to devotees residing at the ashram.

After Swami left, Robert sent a telegram to our taxi driver, Gopal, about 10:30 a.m. telling him to come and fetch us. In the afternoon, he also telephoned several times but could get no answer. It was now 7:30 p.m. in the evening, and we were sitting on the steps of the round house hostel. A taxi pulled up and asked if we needed a ride. We thought maybe we should go because we felt that Gopal did not receive our telegram or else he would have come by now. A lady who was traveling with us mentioned that Baba doesn't like devotees to travel at night and we ought to arrive at our destination while it was still daylight. Our desire to get to Bangalore was so great that we ignored her warning and departed in the taxi.

So, Baba taught us another lesson. It began to rain so hard that we had to pull off the road and wait, not once but several times. We were caught in a downpour, and it was completely dark. A city girl like me had never experienced open country without lights shining from somewhere, even if it was miles away. It was so dark, and visibility on the road was very poor. This was our third trip to India in April, and it never rained at this time of the year, usually. It is summer drought time. Our young driver looked frightened and inexperienced. All three of us prayed to Swami for help. He answered our prayers, and, we arrived safely, but very late.

When I opened our suitcase, another unexpected surprise. We had forgotten that the suitcase was on top of the taxi. It was made of cloth and not waterproof. The rain seeped through onto the black lining of the suitcase, and large black stains ran onto Robert's "whites," and my white slip and choli. It is strange that only the white clothes were stained, even though they were mingled with our other colored clothing. My beautiful white and gold silk wedding sari was the second article from the top. I felt a surge of panic, glancing quickly for stains. As I examined the sari, I realized that this beautiful sari could have been ruined, but it was OK. Even though we disobeyed Him, He protected us. His Love knows no boundary.

The stains were very symbolic of what happens to our souls when we do not heed the words of the Lord. What a vivid learning experience. We would never forget those large black and gray stains. We must always remember and understand that the Lord's words are serious. He gives advice for a valid reason. In our case, the reason was simple; it was dangerous to travel at night in India.

The following morning, Sunday we went to Brindavan. There were bhajans sung continuously throughout the day. The rumors started that Baba was going to Ooty.

Nothing compares with the uniqueness of the game,

"Follow the Lord." The only certainty was His unpredictability. No one ever really knows what He will do, but nevertheless the expectant chase begins. One finds oneself making taxi arrangements, hotel accommodations, plane reservations, all based on "if" Baba leaves. And it is interesting to note how hotels, taxis, and planes all accept the script and timing of Sai Baba as completely normal. There is a calm steadiness, an inner certainty that "God knows and supports all, both great and small," that is ingrained in the Indian culture, and is displayed in these sort of outwardly indefinite circumstances.

The name of 'Ooty' was music to our ears. Our first-year wedding anniversary was April 17, and how exciting it would be for us to spend our anniversary at Ooty, as did our friends Jan and Janice for their one year anniversary.

Previously when we traveled with Swami, most of the permanent devotees traveled with Him too. Only this year everyone was asking for His permission before going. There was definitely a strong message coming from Sai Baba, to all of us to take our connection with Him more seriously. He wanted us to stop acting like irresponsible children. We are His children but there comes a time when even children must grow up and be responsible for their own actions. Mother Sai was pushing us out of the nest. It was time for a mature relationship.

We too must get Baba's permission. This could be accomplished in several ways. Some people He permits to ask openly in darshan, others ask in their hearts. Some give a "Yes/No" note, and if the answer is "Yes," Sai Baba will take the note in darshan. We usually observe and follow the behavior of the permanent devotees. They have had more exposure to Sai Baba's physical presence, and most of them are keenly aware of what behavior is appropriate in the House of the Lord. If you are ever in doubt about some matter you can ask for advice at the accommodation and public relations desk at either ashram, Prashanti Nilayam or Brindavan.

Robert wrote a note to Baba, asking for permission to go to Ooty with Him and during darshan Swami read the note. He told Robert, *"Yes."* This was Sunday and by Tuesday afternoon, the rumors of Sai's trip to Ooty were gathering momentum. He was supposed to leave on Wednesday morning.

Since we were blessed by Baba the year before to travel with Him, Robert decided to ask Swami if we could join his motorcade to Ooty on Wednesday morning. Robert had a "Yes/No" note. During darshan on Tuesday Baba walked directly in front of Robert, but did not take the note. So the answer was "No"; it was definitely a time for us to be grateful for the grace we had already received.

After darshan, Baba went to inspect the construction of Trayee Brindavan, His new home. We waited, because we wanted to see Swami and get His car darshan. The devotees lined the side of the road, but Baba's car stopped at the boys' hostel. Swami got out, and I noticed that Robert was standing in front of Baba's car. He suddenly remembered the note, in his pocket.

Quickly Robert took it out and Swami walked over and took it. Then He disappeared into the hostel. Sai Baba gave us permission to join His motorcade after all.

It was now 7:30 a.m. and we were still waiting under the tree for Swami to pass. Robert shouted, "Here comes Swami's car." Now, I truly know the ultimate meaning of the saying, "What a sight to behold!" We hastily got out of the taxi to greet Baba as he passed. Baba looked out of His car window, smiled, and gave us a hearty wave. We jumped into the waiting taxi and became the fourth and last car in the motorcade to Ooty.

Shortly after we joined the motorcade, Swami's car stopped, because it had a flat tire! We all laughed, imagine God's car getting a flat tire. Baba's behavior is sometimes very human and can be misleading to skeptics. Dr. Hislop asked Swami, "But skeptics wonder why God should assume human form?" Baba answered, *"Because that is the only way to incarnate the God within man. The Avatar takes the human form and behaves in a human way so that humanity can feel kinship with Divinity. At the same time, he rises to godly heights so that mankind also can aspire to reach God. The realization of the indwelling God as the motivator of life is the task for which Avatars come in human form."*

The very first thing I noticed when I got out of the car was Baba's foot, protruding from the open car door. There is a message in His every action. He was wiggling His toes as if to say, "Rita, come surrender your life to My Lotus Feet."

"If you give up all and surrender to the Lord, He will

229

guard you and guide you. The Lord has come just for this very task, He is declaring that He will do so and that it is the very task that has brought Him here!"

The tire was changed and the flat one was taken to the nearest village for repair. The journey resumed with the three remaining cars.

Without any warning, Swami began speaking to me inside. This raises the question: Is it possible to hear the voice of God speaking inside each of us? Some people hear the voice and believe that the statement is true; others do not hear the voice and question the validity of those who hear. It is only natural for them to question because they have not experienced this aspect of their nature. Sai Baba corrects the confusion and the doubts that exist in the mind and answers this question.

"God is not somewhere away from you, someone distant from you. He is in you. He is before you. He is behind you, beckoning, guiding warning prompting the Inner Voice speaking ever with you, you need not seek Him. He is there ready to respond to the call from your heart. Call on Me. I am always by your side. Believe that Sai Baba is in your heart as your Self, unshakable, full of Love."

Sai began speaking and teaching me within. "When you follow me, you need to be aware of two things. You must be near and keep me in your vision. This is not difficult, because we are driving along a straight flat road. Even though there is a great distance between us, you can still see the white Mercedes." The voice continued as we reach the Bandipur Forest. "Now the countryside is very dense and the incline is straight up. There is one hairpin turn after another. When the road is flat and straight, the distance between us can be greater and you can still see me. Now that we have entered the forest, because of its density, difficulty, and curves, you cannot see me.

"It is the same in your daily life. When everything in your life is smooth and straight, no bumps and jumps, you have greater distance between the times you think of Sai. But when your life becomes tense with difficulties like the thick forest, with severe incline and curves, you must have Sai not ahead of you but right with you. To prepare for these times of need, you must practice during times of calm, visualizing My form and repeating My name. Just because the road is smooth and straight; there is no need for you to become relaxed in your spiritual practice, and allow greater distance between us."

When we approached the middle of the forest, Baba's car turned onto a side road. Sundaram said, "This might be the road to the inner forest! I heard that Baba sometimes stops for lunch at a rest stop here." The driver confirmed, "This is the road." Were we excited! Complete equanimity. All I kept thinking about was the symbolism of traveling with the Lord to the inner forest. This is what we must all do within ourselves, and now we were actually having the opportunity to experience this as a 'live' event, traveling with God to the inner forest.

The road ended at a lovely white and blue cottage. It was nestled in between the forest mountains. The hills were rich with trees, undergrowth, and wild flowers which came to rest in the valley below.

Sai Baba gave us darshan, then retired to the cottage, to have lunch with His invited guests. We sat outside, underneath a large shade tree. It is very important to know the correct protocol when you are traveling with Baba. Since we were not invited guests of Swami's, but allowed by His grace to travel along, we stayed outside. Another lesson is to never impose our own will on the Lord but to follow His direction and be prepared when He calls.

Have you ever heard the sound of silence? I experienced it here, more pronounced than ever before, in the inner forest with Sai. It is a deafening experience. There was a sacred stillness everywhere, as if creation was reverently bowing to its Creator. I felt like a sponge, opening its pores, and absorbing to the greatest capacity. The inner voice said, "This is your center; stay within its peaceful boundaries; don't travel on the periphery."

An hour quickly passed, and we were surprised with lunch. Sai Baba sent Srinivasan with a plate of food for each of us. It was Robert's and my first Indian meal in India. We did not usually eat Indian food because it was too hot for us, but we ate this because it was blessed food, given by the Lord. After an hour and a half for lunch and rest, the trip resumed, each car following in the previous order. The others had caught up with us after getting the tire fixed, so again we were

232

four.

Sai Baba was travelling to Ooty for the opening ceremony on Friday April 13, 1984, of the new Ganesh Temple for the primary school children in the Sathya Sai Baba Vidyavihar.

"Man stands in need of pure intelligence. Once he attains it, he can achieve success in all undertakings. That is why students pray to Ganesh after installing him in a shrine. He grants intelligence by which man can know even beyond the realm of the senses. When any sense or indriya drags man towards certain objects or plans, the intelligence must step in and examine whether they are proper or improper."

We arrived in Ooty. Swami went to the school, and we found accommodation. My memory had served me well - Ooty was just as beautiful as I remembered. So much had happened in our life since the last time we were here. It seemed much longer than five years ago.

At the beginning of each trip to India, I usually announced my arrival to Sai Baba by handing Him in darshan a letter of thanks and a list of questions seeking His help. One of the questions, I asked Baba this time was to teach me to distinguish between my desires and His inner voice? I found that asking for help is not always easy...

I had been tempted not to include this question on my list. I told myself "If you ask for guidance in inner communication, there is a strong possibility that Sai will not communicate with you outwardly." This translates into 'no interview'. "Who wants to miss a chance for an 'interview',," I asked myself. I noted with interest how well I could hear the voice of the "ego" and how difficult it was to hear the voice of God! I wondered why I was hesitating on this question. Then I realized the ego has many ways of keeping us distant from God. To think that getting closer on the inner level might handicap one at the outer lever could be a typical 'ego' ploy.

Baba tells us that there are four basic points for self-inquiry. *"1. The body–What is it? 2. The Body–I am not it? 3. Then, who am I? 4. Well, I am That!*

"KNOW THYSELF. Every schoolboy today knows about the sun, the moon, the stars, about the outermost regions of space; but not even the most encyclopedic scholar knows the answer to the very elementary query, 'Who am I?' 'I' is the most frequently used word; it recurs many times every second in conversation. 'I said,' 'I saw,''I went,' 'I heard,' 'I have this,' 'I am King,' 'I am peasant,' 'I am a child,' 'I am a scholar,' 'I am tall,' 'I am lean'–but who is this 'I' that has these attributes and possessions? The Upanishads declare that the I is not the personalized individual; that is a delusion. It is not limited to the body which it inhabits. It is the most universal of categories, it is the Eternal Absolute, the Overself or Universal Self. It is the Omnipresent Universal Consciousness, the Immortal Existence Universal Knowledge and Absolute Bliss."

I began self-inquiry to see exactly what I was feeling and thinking. I realized that my desire to speak with God in human form was stronger than my desire to speak with God within. The debate in my mind continued. "How long is an interview?

The reply –"An hour if you are lucky".

Next question,–"And how long is inner communication with God?"

"As long as you desire to listen." The reply came promptly, and continued.

"If you can have a continuous dialogue with God every day, why do you choose only one hour?"

"Because I can see Him, listen to Him, speak with Him, and feel His presence, so I'm attached to my physical body and the senses."

Next question, "What is this body? Isn't the body temporary? Is it really your permanent self? Isn't it also possible to use your inner senses for the same pleasure as the outer senses?"

"Yes I know I can visualize God, I can listen to Him, I can speak with Him, and I can feel His presence, all inwardly." I answered.

The dialogue continued–"Anyway, Rita, who is this I?"

"Who am I?

Baba told us in our first interview. *"I am God and you are God. We are both God, only I realize this and you don't!"*

"And what is the purpose of this trip?"

The questions continued. "To realize your own divinity, with the help of Sai Baba. Isn't that just what you asked for in your note, for Baba to increase your awareness and identity with the God within?"

"I'm caught!" The little self (ego) had been caught by the big SELF, the God within. The request for better inner communication went on my list.

One of the most troublesome problems I encountered with inner communication was listening to direction that was contrary to my desires. When there is no desire, there is less difficulty and complete freedom to listen. The stronger the desire, the less likely I am to believe what I am hearing is true.

At Brindavan, I had inwardly asked Sai, how to distinguish between the voice of my ego and the voice of the Atma, since they both seem to use the same voice. Swami said, " Rita, the more intense your desire, the greater chance for error. You are free to listen and have greater accuracy when you have no desire. Like right now, you are having no difficulty hearing me. Use a scale of 1 to 10 and measure the strength of your desire. For example, the desire for an interview with Swami is the maximum strength, say a 10. Therefore, each time, after you measure your desire, find its strength, then compensate by ignoring the desire."

He continued, "Feel with your heart, not your mind, because my instruction comes from 'heart to heart.' When you recognize the truth, there will be no disharmony, only a feeling of unity. Desires in the mind cause feelings of conflict. If you act on the truth from the Atma, you will have peace, a oneness of thought, word, and deed. Rita, observe your desires, in conflict with My Will. I will teach you while you're here."

Baba had begun teaching me on our journey to Ooty.

He told me something through the inner voice concerning day to day events, and then allowed me to experience the message He gave me, giving me proof so I knew whether I was hearing correctly or not correctly. An example: While we were in Ooty, we heard that Sai was going to visit one of the adopted villages the next day. Immediately, the voice within said "You are not to go." Sometimes these instructions are so subtle they are easy to miss. Our personal radar, awareness, has to be finely tuned to receive the inner pulse of communication. Well, that instruction didn't seem too adverse to accept, until the next morning. Along came the temptaion of desire.

It just happened that at darshan I was sitting next to one of the Seva Dal leaders who helped to plan Sai Baba's visit to the village. She leaned over and spoke to me. "Are you coming with Sai to the village program today?" I answered, "I don't think so." (My answer clearly showed I was missing my target.)

The flame of my desire to join Swami visiting the village was increased by the fuel of encouragement from the lady sharing her excitement with me. Her joy and excitement was a pure motive. She didn't know what Swami had said to me yesterday. She continued, "You MUST come. Swami invited ALL the devotees. There will be a grand program given by the villagers." The inner alarm is going 'CONFLICT, CONFLICT, clang, clang etc.'

My desire to go was interfering with my inner instruction. My mind was saying. "Swami didn't give you any reason for not going. What difference does it make, if you go? The lady said ALL the devotees are invited." Inside I yelled, "Help! Swami, Help! I think I've got another 10. Please, Swami, give me another sign before you leave. I do not wish to disobey your instruction if it really is your instruction. Show me the truth."

I felt confident that during darshan Baba would give me the right answer. But as I looked up, I saw His car driving to the door. Baba came out, got into the car....no darshan. I searched, for a clue and was still asking for help while waiting for car darshan. I was on the side where Swami was sitting. As His car passed, my eyes meet His, and within that instant, the message that was transferred was clear. It was a strong, powerful, command...STAY." A sigh of relief echoed through my conflicting mind and body.

Shortly afterwards, we returned to our room and Robert and I became very sick. We had fever, diarrhea, nausea, and weakness. I thought, "Oh, Swami, you rascal. Diarrhea in the village would have been awful!" He certainly got His point across. I reinforced the lesson by telling myself several times that I must unquestionably obey, with or without a reason.

As Robert and I lay sick in bed, the voice whispered, "I will give you darshan at 5:00 p.m. in your room, and you will feel much better." I said, "Thank you, Baba," told Robert, and drifted off to sleep. We awoke at 5:00 p.m. and did feel much much better! Around seven, Maggie and Sundaram knocked on our door. We had

238

sent our taxi driver to pick up both the girls and take them to evening darshan. He told them we were sick, and they came by to check on us and unintentionally delivered another confirmation to me.

We immediately asked about darshan. It was canceled because of rain, they said, but Baba invited everyone in for bhajans. Sundaram said, "One strange thing happened during bhajans. Baba had a medal on a chain, just like the one He made for you, Rita, and started swinging it in the air."

I said, "Did you by any chance know what time that happened?" Sundaram said, "Yes, I do, it was 5:00 p.m. I had just checked my watch." She knew nothing about Swami telling me earlier that we would receive His darshan at 5 p.m.

There are millions of souls on earth who also listen for their inner guidance, but do not have God, Himself, physically giving proof of His communication. We are so richly blessed to know that God is in human form on earth today. He surrounds us with signs pointing the way to truth. It is like a treasure hunt. We must carefully search for His signs along the path, showing us the correct route to the gift of Eternal Life, buried deep within the chambers of our own real self.

"If you take one step toward me, I take ten steps toward you. Remember that with every step, you are nearing God. And when you take one step toward Him, God takes ten toward you. There is no halting place in this pilgrimage; it is one continuous journey, through day and night; through valley and desert; through tears and smiles, through death

*and birth, through tomb and womb. When the road ends
and the goal is gained, the pilgrim finds that he has traveled
only from himself to himself, that the way was long and
lonesome; but, the God that led him, was all the while in
him, around him, within, and beside him! He Himself was
always Divine. His yearning to merge in God was but the
sea calling the Ocean! Man loves, because He is love! He
craves for melody and harmony. He seeks Joy for, He is
Joy. He thirsts for God, for, he is composed of God, and
he cannot exist without Him."*

Sai Baba drives me far beyond what I think are my
limits. Like Arjuna's charioteer, He gets more mileage
than seems possible out of one tank of circumstances,
using each bump and curve in the road. Even when He
burns my rubber and overheats my engine, His ratio of
input to output is magnificent.

Do we each have a personal God? The answer is
yes! Our personal God resides within each of us. It is
the voice of the Atma. Each of us has a personalized
program for learning. God teaches us on our own level
of understanding, and with the tools already familiar to
us. Only a personal God would know my level of
understanding, my frame of reference, and communicate
His knowledge so I can receive His divine wisdom.

Swami communicated another message to me which
was bitter to swallow. As we were traveling through
the mountains going to Ooty, He said, "You will not
return to Brindavan traveling with me, nor will you get
an interview this trip." How I disliked hearing those
words, especially after the struggle I already described

about adding that question to my list. My ego only wanted to hear pleasure, not the pain. But I knew that one does not exist without the other. The mind likes to reject the unwanted instructions and wants to hang onto the wish-fulfilling dreams, facing reality only when it is forced. So I still hoped that what I had heard was wrong, but I was prepared to accept the Truth of those words. I knew my desire was a 10, and I could feel peace in my heart when I accepted His statement as true. I had passed the test; that He had taught me. Thank God.

Even though Swami had told me we would not be traveling on our return trip with Him, we made a group effort to try in case I misheard. We knew that Swami was leaving for Brindavan the next morning, and we planned to arrive early for darshan in the hope that we could travel with Him. I set the alarm clock for 5 a.m.

In the morning, I awoke at 5:30 a.m. and wondered why the alarm had not rung. I examined the clock and found that I 'unconsciously' had set the digital clock at p.m. instead of a.m. We missed Swami, and we learned later that He took a different route back and attended to some business along the way.

The following day, Robert and I made an appointment with Sai's photographer in Bangalore to select a few pictures to take home. Swami had just recently approved a picture of himself to be placed in the new mandir, and we were able to get a large copy of this photo, a memorable keepsake for the up-coming opening.

The morning that Robert brought the photo to darshan

for Sai to sign, we both had a similar experience. Robert sat quietly, closing his eyes, turning inward, before darshan. The inner message he received was clear and simple. Baba wanted us to grow-up from children to adults. He wanted us to have a more mature relationship with him. A child asks God to fill his wants and desires. The adult only wants what he needs to kill his desires. Baba is saying that it is time to take Him seriously and practice His teachings.

That morning Baba allowed Robert to have padnamaskar, signed our picture, and gave him a very big smile. He felt that Baba was affirming the inner message. Strangely, I received the same inner message, at darshan, confirming it completely.

A few days before the Grand Opening of Trayee Brindavan, His new residence, Swami told a few men and women from the darshan line to *"go."* Robert was one of them. As we all walked towards the gate and entered the garden, we could see the beautiful new residence. I wondered what this unexpected pleasure was all about? Baba had told me 'no interview' so why were we here? There were about nine Western ladies, other than myself, all permanent residents, and two gents plus Robert from the United States.

In lines along the driveway were men and women villagers who had worked on building Swami's new residence–ladies on the left side and men on the right. Sai opened the trunk of his car and took out gifts for the villagers. The trunk of His car reminded me of the old-time peddler who kept a special item in His wagon for everyone. It was a magical moment. He gave each of the men a new dothi and the ladies a new sari. He made many trips to the car trunk and delighted us all with His endless stream of gifts.

Swami returned from the car with another stack of saris in His arms, this time giving them to the Western ladies. It was amazing how complimentary the color of each person's sari was to their hair and skin tones. On His last trip from the trunk, He carried a stack of white envelopes in His hands. They were invitations to the Trayee Brindavan Opening. He handed one to each of the ladies, then proceeded to the men. He handed Mr. Erving Goldstein an invitation and said "Lunch," and passed by Robert.

"Where's mine?" asked Robert?

Sai replied, *"Your wife has yours!"*

Robert's ego plummeted. Swami had always treated Robert's and my relationship as very Indian, allowing Robert to have the dominant role. This was definitely a "women's lib" action from Baba, and I loved it! The invitations explained the purpose of this wee gathering.

Swami certainly caught us off-guard with His surprise. It never entered my mind that we needed to have an invitation to attend. We were also puzzled as to why Swami told Mr. Goldstein "lunch." We looked at the invitation repeatedly, but never discovered until the following day that on the back was an invitation to lunch with Sai Baba and an evening Cultural Program.

The Official Opening festival began. Everything had

a fresh coat of paint and was decorated with flags, flowers, and streamers. The entrance walk-way was adorned with beautiful designs made out of flower petals. There were garlands of flowers swinging from two magnificent hand–carved, large wooden doors that open into Baba's new home. A ribbon was stretched over the entrance for Swami to cut. The marching band students were dressed in colorful uniforms. All the ladies were in their finest saris, and the men wore their finest shirts and new bright white cottons. The priests were performing a Yajna, praying for us to overcome evil tendencies. Many of the guests were seated here, under a big red and white striped tent which gave shade from the hot sun.

Since married couples shared an invitation, they were seated first. We were fortunate to get good seats, especially Robert. There were a group of photographers standing by the Trayee Brindavan entrance, and Robert decided to join them. He became the unofficial photographer for the U.S.

Baba's car followed the parade. As Swami stepped out of the car, He was greeted by a special group of devotees who lined the walkway. Swami slowly made His way toward the entrance for the ribbon-cutting ceremony. That officially began the day's activities.

Sai Baba entered His new residence with the priests chanting behind Him, followed by the photographers recording this event on film. Sai Baba was cleansing and blessing each room of this new temple of God. Robert was allowed inside through the grace of Sai to witness the event.

244

Afterwards, Sai had ice cream cups distributed to the thousands of guests. It was summer and very hot, and yet the ice cream was firm and cold. Sai was so happy in giving us a party, His joy was infectious.

Sai's students came towards Baba with their arms filled with gifts for some of the men. They were zipped leather cases, filled with a notebook, Vibhuthi, pen, and a picture of Sai with the inscription "Call on me, and I am always by your side." Sai Baba was tossing them to the men. He called to Robert, *"Do you want one?"*

"Yes, Sai," says Robert, and Swami tossed it to him. Every occasion and festival held in Sai Baba's ashrams included acts of service. Feeding the poor, was the next event on the agenda. The poor from the surrounding villages gathered and were fed by Swami and His helpers, the Seva Dals.

"Look about for chances to relieve, rescue, or resuscitate. Train yourselves that you may render help quickly and well. Seva–Service is the most paying form of austerity, the most satisfying, and the most pleasurable! It springs out of love and it scatters love in profusion. It plants a seed on stone and is delighted to see it sprout! Plant it with love, and the seed will discover love inside the stone and draw sustenance therefrom.

"It is the inner joy, the love that you radiate, that is important. Mere sentiment and sympathy are of no use; they must be regulated by intelligence. Shower cheer on the sad; soothe those who have lost the way; close your eyes to the faults of others, but, keep them open to discover your own. All these are hard jobs. Practice

alone can make you perfect–practice, not only in items of service, but in meditation on the Divine. Prayer beads and meditation will render you more and more efficient in the field of service."

Swami has taught us the importance and inner significance of seva, or service to others. Service is the very fiber of the Sai Baba organization. The members weave with their helping hands to make a cloth of love to wrap around the poor, needy and suffering of our world. It is the highest form of spiritual worship that we can offer to God. Swami explains the role of service and its inner meaning for His devotees.

"The responsibilities of the Seva Dal (the Service Wing of the Sai Organization) are of a high order. They have to lead the members and through them all mankind, along the path of spiritual discipline which takes the individual from the position 'I' to the position 'We.' This has given the Seva Dal the importance it deserves. One can realize it only when one delves deeply into the inner significance. You have to sublimate all work as worship, and try to fill every moment of your lives with that outlook. Only then can you justify your membership in this organization.

"Through activity, man attains purity of consciousness. In fact, man has to welcome activity with this end in view. And why strive for a pure consciousness? Imagine a well with polluted and muddy water, so that the bottom of the well cannot be seen. When the water is cleansed and made clear, then the floor can be seen; similarly, within man's heart, deep down in his consciousness, we have the Self. But it can be cognized only when the

consciousness is clarified. Your imagings, your inferences, your judgements and prejudices, your passions, emotions, and egoistic desires muddy the consciousness and make it opaque. How, then, can you become aware of the Self that is at the very base? Through seva rendered without any desire to placate one's ego and with only the well-being of others in view, it is possible to cleanse the consciousness and have the Self revealed.

"Therefore, for whose sake are you performing seva? You are doing seva for your own sake. You are engaged in seva in order that you may discard the allurements of your ego in order to know yourself and to get the answer to the question that torments you, namely, "Who am I." You do not serve others — you serve yourselves; you do not serve the world — you serve your own best interests.

"You may ask: How is it possible to transcend the ego through seva? By saturating the seva with love, work can be transformed into worship. When the work is offered to God, it gets sanctified into worship. This makes it free from ego. It is also freed from the earthly desire for success and the earthly fear of failure. You feel that when you have done the work as best as you can, your worship is accomplished; now it is for Him who has accepted the worship to confer what He considers best. This attitude will make the work unattached. Regular practice of this discipline will render the consciousness clear and pure."

The evening music program brought the day to close, and it also ended our trip to India. We left the cultural program to catch our plane to Bombay. It had been an unusual trip, spiritually significant for us both. We were tired as we departed, but were glowing inside, filled with Baba's love.

In Bombay the following morning I awoke feeling very ill. I had a fever, chills, sweats, diarreah, etc. Robert sent for the hotel doctor. The doctor seemed to think that I had a bacterial infection in my colon, possibly coming from the raw milk served yesterday at the luncheon. Robert and I had eaten the same food except for the milk. I foolishly thought that since I was eating with Swami everything was blessed and would give me no ill effects, so I took a few sips of the unpasteurized milk. I suddenly felt so sick that I couldn't even imagine what condition I would be in if I drank the whole glass. Well, Swami taught me another important lesson. Do not confuse 'grace' with practicality; and I had.

Our trip home was the worst travel experience we had encountered in our journeys to India. Since our invitation to the Trayee Brindavan Opening was the day of our scheduled flight, we had changed our flight by one day. We were on stand-by but Air India felt certain we would get a seat. I spent the day pumping in fluids and medication, but I felt like dying.

Our flight departed around 1 a.m. Robert went to the airport early to check-in since I was so weak. Later we got our tickets, boarded the plane, stowed our luggage, and started to sit down when our names were called over the speaker to immediately come up front. The first thought parents have is, "Did something happen to our children?"

We were two innocent lambs being led astray. The Air India official said we needed to leave the plane but would not give us a reason. He kept talking and walking as we followed him off the plane. We never became wise until we saw a very well-dressed Indian couple pass us and board the plane. We had been deboarded but still given no explanation. How do you stay detached and not lose your center? We blew it. I was too sick to argue, but the tears flooded my eyes.

I couldn't believe what was happening. After all the effort it took for us to get here, and now we didn't even have a ticket. The Air India official sent us to an office to wait for someone to explain. We waited three hours. We couldn't leave since we had no tickets. After the three-hour wait an official entered, gave us our outdated tickets, and referred us to someone in the Bombay office downtown. We also had no luggage.

This was Thursday, and it was the next Monday before we received a flight home. We were so shocked at the unfair treatment we received. Every official sent us to someone else. No-one was sympathetic or concerned about our needs. They would not reimburse us for all our added expenses–taxis, hotel, meals, and clothing. Robert was angry and also late for work. What a leela!

When we finally arrived in New York to claim our luggage, it was damaged! The details of this horror filled a six-page, typewritten letter to the President of

Air India. He did not even have the courtesy to reply. Since the airline was from a foreign country, there was nothing we could do to recover our losses. All four of our trips had been on Air India, but that looked like the last.

Sai says, "Detachment gives peace even amidst troubles. This world is like a shining drop of water that collects on a lotus leaf. It quivers and shakes without being steady. Heaps of attachments fill the life of man. Trouble and sorrow constitute the screen on which the world shows itself.

"As a drop of water on a lotus leaf disappears in no time, even so, we should know that our life is transient and will disappear very much like that and in no time. The world is full of sorrow, and the human body is full of disease. Our life is full of turbulent thoughts and is like a dilapidated house. Under these conditions, according to Shankara, it is possible to live in a peaceful manner by following the divine path and getting over all our worldly attachments. So long as one does not know who he is, one cannot escape these sorrows. So long as one does not realize the Eswara or the presence of God in every thing, one cannot escape this sorrow. So long as one does not understand that to be born, to grow, to live, and to die is only for one purpose and that is to understand the nature of Atma Tatwa and is finally extinguished in the Atma Tatwa, or divine principle. This verse conveys that the divine principle is the pond or the lake, that maya, or illusion, is the bunch of leaves, and that the jiva, or individual soul, comes out as the lotus flower in this pond of Atma, or God. This lotus spreads the

fragrance of many good qualities. While spreading
such fragrance, even the water in the pond becomes one
with the Atma Tatwa. The drops of water which come
out of the pond of Atma come to the leaves of the lotus
and go back to the Atma. This going back to the source is
what is contained as an essence in this verse. In the
infinity of the Atma. the jiva comes as the lotus because
maya spreads in the form of leaves. The jiva which is like
the lotus spreads the fragrance of the good qualities which
can be ascribed to the jiva tatwa".

There were two additional experiences that helped me
in my search for better inward communication.

One Sunday at Mass, the priest told a story about
Joan of Arc. Joan was condemned to death because she
heard the voice of God instructing her. While Joan was
in prison, condemned to death, she was visited by a
friend. He pleaded with her, "Joan, if you will only tell
the officials that the voice you hear is your imagination,
you will not die."

Joan replied, "It is my imagination." Before his joy
could take form, she continued, "It is my imagination,
because the voice that I hear can only speak through
imagination." I frequently would ask Baba, "Is this
my imagination or your voice?" This story of Joan
helped me to understand the role of imagination.

I never really thought about it, but unless we use
our imagination, there would be no inner voice of God
to hear. We certainly can't see God and His mouth
expressing these words. We imagine that He lives
within us. Instead of restraining my imagination after

251

this experience, I allowed it more freedom of expression. It helped. 'Just imagine what God is telling you', is the key.

Another source of help came from a book that Catherine Bracey suggested I read, "Practicing the Presence of God", by Brother Lawrence, written in the sixteen hundreds. Brother Lawrence's story is about a monk with simple wisdom who felt the constant companionship of God. His story taught me how to have a continuous dialogue with the Lord.

There is even a Baba story involved in our attempt to locate this book. We checked the book stores in India before we departed, but were unable to locate it. Nothing in Catherine's book itself suggested where to purchase it or where it was printed, so we decided to check in the U.S. We did, but without success.

Almost a year later, Robert was at his company's credit union and noticed the book sitting on an employee's desk. (This Avatar is certainly unconventional!) The woman was really sweet and gave Robert her copy and ordered more books from the Unitarian Church. I had forgotten about the little book, but Swami never forgets.

FAMILY

"How is your son?", or "How is your mother?" asks Sai sometimes in the darshan line. Parents and children alike are most pleased when Swami inquires about the family. On some occasions, Sai is referring to our spiritual family. *"Truth is father, Love is mother, Wisdom is son, Peace is daughter, and Devotion is brother."*

His concern is genuine, as if He is a family member, not a distant relative or friend who inquires only to be polite. He is an active family member who shares in our grief, feels with our heartache, rejoices in our good fortune and most importantly helps, guides, loves, heals, cares, and protects our family flocks.

Our family is His family. Your family is His family. Every devotee in the world shares this in common, regardless of the God-form you worship. This relationship exists between Sri Sathya Sai Baba and our family.

God-worshipping people around the world sometimes question this as truth, but being a Baba devotee has made the obscure obvious, and our beliefs a reality. We, devotees know it to be true, because of Swami's words and actions. God is a personal family member.

We have heard so many stories from people who meet Sai Baba in person for the first time and without being told, He relates facts concerning their life and family members as if He participates in their daily activities, feeling and thinking exactly the same as they do. In fact, He proves that He is Omnipresent.

I knew when I became a devotee and surrendered my life to God, He was responsible for protecting and guiding me. But I was not prepared or aware to the extent of God's involvement with my family. Each and every responsibility of mine became His.

He is the Doer, and I'm His instrument. This doesn't mean that He performs the work and I sit by and watch. No, I try to use every available means known in society to correct a problem. If there is nothing else that I can do, I surrender it consciously, to Him. The more that I am able to surrender, the more He does, and the more I can serve Him.

These are some examples of how Sai Baba has protected and helped our family, and is solving and resolving our family problems. Baba has said, *"God's grace is like insurance; it will help you in your time of need without any limit."* It's the best insurance policy available today!

Carl, Carol's husband, was having problems with the illness of drug abuse. During my 1983 trip to India, I wrote Sai a note and gave Him their picture on the plane from Hyderabad asking for His help. They had been struggling with this problem for the past eight years.

Sai's grace seemed to work miracles during the year following our trip. Carl accomplished behavioral changes that all previous attempts failed. He went through an extensive drug treatment program successfully and returned to college and finished his degree. It was such a proud moment for Carl's parents and us.

Carl had worked day and night, struggling to achieve a degree. He held a job, attended class, studied, and controlled his desire to drink, throughout all this additional stress. My daughter, Carol shouldered much of the responsibility while Carl attended school. She gave the needed financial help by working, plus caring for their daughter and home. Equally important was her emotional and mental support. I'll never forget the joy their accomplishments gave to us. They applied themselves, and with God's Grace, WON!

"Above all, try to win grace by reforming your habits, reducing your desires, and refining your higher nature. One step makes the next one easier; that is the excellence of the spiritual journey. At each step, your strength and confidence increase, and you get bigger and bigger installments of grace."

After graduation, Carl found a good position, earning enough income that could support the purchase of a home. They had no savings, but God worked it out.

They moved into a new home without any down payment, no closing costs, and low interest! Baba is the greatest employer. His Company "perks", and fringe benefits are out of this world!

* * *

Our son Craig announced to us in September 1984, that he was going to India to see Sai Baba. We knew that Craig had organized a trip to Australia to see his old friends, but this additional trip to India was a complete surprise!

Craig had not openly talked about his faith and devotion to Baba. It existed, but in a very subtle manner. He never attended any of the Center functions and read very little of Sai's teachings. He would write Sai often, which was my strongest clue that something underneath was brewing.

We as parents never know when Sai is going to call our children. It is indeed the responsibility of the Lord, and no amount of parental pushing will speed up the process. In most cases, it can only cause delay. Robert and I knew that it was our dream come true.

Craig waved good-by as he boarded the plane, and my mind was filled with parental concern and doubts. This son was no child; he was a man of 26 years. Why am I feeling as if he's a five-year-old going to school for the first time? Will he ever get through Bombay's airport alone? Did I prepare him for the culture shock of India? Will he be able to relate to Sai Baba? Will this trip deepen his relationship or confuse him? What will he do if he has to live in the halls at the ashram? How could a young man from America with a comfortable lifestyle, practically spoon-fed, ever relate to India? Robert looked at me, smiled and said, "Rita, the mother instinct must 'let go!'"

His words were perfect. How difficult it is to turn-off motherhood. You spend your whole life caring for your children's needs, and when they grow up you are supposed to stop. I remember reading that Sai's mother, Easwaramma, also worried about her son. She, too, had difficulty detaching from her role as mother.

Craig's first letter from India arrived at our home on Christmas Eve. I had promised Robert that I would not read the letter until he was at home with me. We were both anxious to hear about Craig's trip. The letter couldn't have pleased us more. Craig loved India, easily adjusted to the ashram life, and Sai Baba showered him with love and attention. I chuckled to myself . . . still being spoon-fed, only Indian style!

Craig also received our first letter on Christmas Eve. His letter brought a message of joy, and ours sent a message of sorrow. We told Craig that his grandfather was dying of cancer. Living in the apartment next to Craig was the Alden family, Gayle, Sylvia, and their 19 year old son, Chuck. They adopted Craig as part of the family and helped him adjust to Prasanthi. They also came to his aid, helping to ease the sad news about his grandfather.

* * *

In October 1984 my father discovered he had cancer of the colon and liver. It seemed like an unfortunate

257

time to receive news of impending death. My parents were going to celebrate their 50th wedding anniversary in a few short weeks. We had planned a Mass and reception for family and friends. It was to be a time of joyous celebration.

The doctor told them to postpone the operation until after their anniversary. It took great strength for my mother and father to go on with the celebrations, even though Dad's illness was terminal. Somehow they would manage, and they did. Their strength came from their deep faith in God.

A few days after their anniversary, Dad's colon became blocked and emergency surgery was performed. Again, Divine timing. As mother and I sat across from the surgeon, we very much wanted to hear that the news was hopeful, but the prognosis was not good. My father had cancer in the small intestine, the abdomen, the colon, and in 50% of the liver. The colon was so inflamed and cancerous that the surgeon had to give my father a colostomy. His death was only a matter of time.

Thanksgiving, Christmas, and New Year's Day passed. Dad's health went from bad to worse . . . his large frame shriveled. He couldn't eat, and lost forty-six pounds. My mother was so depressed that she lost thirty-five pounds from worry.

I constantly called on Swami for the courage to help my parents through these troublesome days. I prayed that if it was His will to please heal my father and give my mother the strength she needed.

My parents were devout Catholics and felt very

close to Jesus. They couldn't understand my relationship with Sai Baba nor the concept of "God in human form," especially in someone other than Jesus. When I spoke about Sai Baba, I could see the fear in their eyes, especially my father's . . . so I remained silent. They actually knew very little about Baba or my trips to India.

Meanwhile, on Christmas Day at Prasanthi, Craig had a front row seat. As Sai Baba approached him, he held up a note asking for Sai to help his grandfather.. Sai refused the note but made Vibhuthi for Craig and gave him padnamaskar.

Craig sent home some of the Vibhuthi. It arrived mid-January. After taking the Vibhuthi, Dad's weight stabilized. They used the Vibhuthi because I told them of its miraculous power to heal. They had nothing to lose – they were desperate.

One afternoon in January, I was meditating, mostly talking with Baba. It seemed as if I heard Him saying that Robert and I should come for a visit in March and November for his 60th Birthday in the year of '85.

I replied, "But Sai, my father is dying of cancer. How can I come in March?" The voice replied, "Don't worry, I'll take care of your father." Immediately, we arranged for airline tickets leaving March 1st.

In February my father received an unusual phone call. The surgeon called and suggested that Dad have another operation to reconnect the colon and reverse the colostomy. Dad had not seen this surgeon for several months and to have him call without any prior contact was unusual. They felt the call was a sign from God, they prayed and decided to have the second operation.

This time after surgery, the doctor was hopeful. He was smiling from ear to ear. He said that the colon was much much better. He removed the cancerous tumor and reconnected the bowel. As far as he could tell, all the cancer was removed from the colon. He further stated that the cancer in the liver, intestine, and abdomen looked to be benign. A few days later, this was confirmed by the tests. The doctors were amazed! They were further astonished by Dad's quick recovery after four hours of major surgery. We took Dad home after one week, three days before we left for India . . . "Divine timing." Indeed!

At Prashanti, Sai Baba gave us an interview. I held up my parent's picture and asked, "Sai, did you cure my father of cancer?" Baba slapped me on the shoulder and replied, *"I sure did!"* I will never forget the thrill of my Father telling me he had cured my father, and in such a natural fatherly way!

Sai Baba's love and grace had spilled over into the lives of my children, and now this same expansive love had reached out to touch the lives of my parents. I read many times about Sai Baba's miracles of healing, never realizing that someday it would include my father. His frail, sickly form soon blossomed into his old healthy self. The comparison seemed unbelievable; Sai Baba made it believable.

As I wrote this chapter, my father had just completed a physical examination at the hospital. The doctors reported that the X-rays showed nothing new since his surgery three years ago. There was no new cancer growth!

* * *

My daughter Joan, is the youngest member of our family. Two weeks after we arrived home from our 1984 India trip, she had an automobile accident. Joan had a beautiful face and did some part-time modeling. She had left home using the family car to go to a modeling job. The accident occurred at the corner of our street. As she turned the corner, she reached for a glass of water which was sitting on the floor, trying to prevent it from spilling. The car went out of control, hit a post, and Joan's face went through the windshield.

I could hear her screaming as she came through the door. She was bleeding profusely from her mouth. I tried calming her fears, assuring her it will be OK. as I led her to the bathroom to cleanse the wound. I sent Sai an SOS. Her teeth came through her chin, laying it wide open, and her face was badly cut. Oh, Baba, I thought, it's her face! I packed the wound in ice and called my brother-in-law, who is a dentist.

Jack told me his best friend was one of the finest plastic surgeons in St. Louis. Joan was given extraordinary care. The surgeon met us at the hospital, leaving his office filled with patients. She had thirty stitches in her mouth, chin, and cheek. Between Sai and the surgeon, the scar on her face is not noticeable. It's hard to believe today that her face was in such bad shape.

Our new car was totaled. When I saw the car, the broken telephone post hanging by a twig, and the falling electrical wires around the car, I knew Sai had come to our rescue again.

*   *   *

When Craig came home from his first trip to India, he announced that he would join us for Sai Baba's 60th birthday celebrations. It was such joy having our son with us for this auspicious occasion. Craig was planning on staying at Prasanthi until the end of January, but Sai had another surprise and kept him until May.

This is a love story – a wedding conceived in heaven and arranged by God. His letter came on a January day, early in 1986. I waited to open it until Robert came home. I was so glad I did. This news was such fun to share. The letter began with "Dear Mom and Dad, I suggest you both sit down, I've got some news. I've met a girl whom I think I will marry. She is Patricia Narinesingh, an Indian girl from Trinidad.

"After you left Prasanthi, I became friends with Peter and Malcolm Narinesingh, Patricia's two brothers. After Christmas, Patricia surprised her brothers and arrived at Whitefield. I was introduced a day later. The leela all started with a red velvet picture album."

262

It seems that Craig took fantastic pictures of Swami and put them in a red album. He took it to darshan, Swami held it, looked through some of the pictures, and blessed it. Craig showed the album to Patricia, and she loved it. (Patricia told me months later that the album was breathtaking, blissfull, fantastic, and words could not describe how it made her feel. I chuckled to myself, her words of expression were those of a newly wed in love.)

Later that day, Craig sat under the big darshan tree at Brindavan, reflecting on Patricia's interest in the album. He decided that he would make her a smaller album with Baba's pictures. Suddenly, Baba's voice inside said, "No, give her the album Swami touched."

Craig replied, "Baba, I can't. I love it too much!" Again, the voice said, "Give her the album Swami touched." Craig thought, "I wouldn't mind so much if I gave it to a member of my own family."

Baba's voice said, "Give her the big album, it will not leave your family." Craig had just met Patricia and was struggling with this message, but reluctantly obeyed four days later. Several nights went by. Then Craig was awakened and heard the voice say, "Write Swami a note asking if this is the girl you will marry?" Swami took the note in darshan and told him, **"Yes"**.

By now, Craig thought it was time to confide in Patricia. She too, was feeling that Craig was special, but she would do nothing unless Swami approved. Their marriage was being arranged, Indian-style.

263

In our 1983 interview, Sai refused Craig's selection of a marriage partner and told us he would find him a good girl. Craig prayed to him often for a wife who was a devotee – a girl who had the same moral values and would stay home and care for their children. He was having great difficulty finding this type of person in St. Louis. In an interview in 1984, Sai told Patricia that He would find her a good boy for a husband and blessed her wedding sari. It seems that Sai was setting the stage for this scene in His play.

We also discovered after the children arrived home, that both of the fathers, respectively, wrote Sai Baba a note surrendering their son and daughter to him. It was given to Baba in secret. Rana, Patricia's father, sent a letter with her this trip. Robert gave his letter to Sai while sitting in the darshan line in November, the 60th Birthday.

On the 4th of February, Baba called Patricia and her eldest brother Malcolm in for an interview. Baba asked her, *"Where is your husband?"*

She replied, "I'm not married, but there is this boy who wants to marry me." Swami was so much like Shiva playing the role of the father. He sounded like any father whose daughter came home saying those words.

Swami continued, *"Where are your parents?"*

"They're in Canada," she said.

"Where is this boy?" asked Sai.

"He's sitting in the darshan line."

"What's his name?"

"Craig Bruce," she replied.

"Where's he from?"

"America," said Patricia.

"Americans very bad. One wife this year, and another the next."

The questions continued, *"What does he do?"*

She said, "He wants to teach."

Baba said, *"What does he know how to teach? What is he telling you?"*

Swami's questions and statement about Americans bringing new wives year after year is certainly enough to scare any girl. It was a difficult interview for Patricia because she received no answers, only questions – questions for her to think about. She realized that Baba wanted her to seek out her own true feelings concerning marriage to Craig.

Swami traveled to Madras. There was an early-morning darshan and Patricia had arrived late, crowds of people were already there, but by some great fortune, she was given a seat in front. She noticed Craig, also in front. She had a perfect view when Swami came to him. Craig was holding a picture of Patricia and himself. Baba came right over, took their picture, holding it in both of his hands, staring for some time, while displaying the most beautiful grin. It was the sign that Patricia had sought – Swami's approval.

Meanwhile, back home, the Narinesinghs and the Bruces, through many phone conversations, became the best of friends. We all wanted to go to India, but decided to surrender to Sai's will. We sent Craig a letter and a cable to give to Baba, asking permission to come for the wedding. To make absolutely certain of Sai Baba's decision, He would have to say to Craig or Patricia, "Tell your parents to come." Craig took our letter and cable to darshan, and Swami took them, but gave no reply. Then Craig asked Him in the darshan line, and there was no reply. We waited and waited. We even received from TWA Frequent Flyer Bonus Program two coupons for 50% off any ticket, and they fly from St. Louis to Bombay. Was that a sign that we were going or a test of our surrender?

It was a test of surrender. Did each parent really give their daughter and son to Sai Baba? We stayed home, and Sai Baba guided them, blessed them, and provided for every need.

Craig asked Swami for permission to marry Patricia Narinesingh on Sunday, April 27, at St. Francis Xavier Cathedral in Bangalore. Swami said, *"Yes, yes, very happy, very happy."* Then he blessed Craig with a pat on the head. Patricia and Craig were both raised as Catholics.

Swami, our matchmaker, did a wonderful job. I'm told that Sai Baba doesn't usually mix races. But Patricia is a good mixture of both cultures. Her mother

Rosemary was Catholic, and her father Rana, a Hindu. She was blessed with knowledge of both faiths. She was born and lived in Trinidad in the West Indies. Again although she is Indian her lifestyle and personality are American. She fits into our family snugly, like a softskin kid glove.

Both sets of parents, Rosemary and Rana, Rita and Robert, are a mixture of the East and the West. The marriage of these two families symbolizes, synthesizes, and syncretizes these two diverse cultures.

Their wedding represented the true meaning of Catholicism – universality. Devotees from around the world joined together to participate in this wedding celebration. They all took their assigned roles from the play director of the universe, Sri Sathya Sai Baba. Richard Kaplowitz became the father of the bride, and his two loving daughters were the flower girls. An Indian couple, very close friends, Vanitha and Vijay Kumar, became the maid-of-honor and the best man. Swami kept the theme alive – even the wedding party represented a balanced combination of East and West.

It was a beautiful wedding day. The bride and bridegroom dressed for the Wedding Day Festivities came to Brindavan for Sunday morning bhajans and darshan. Patricia wore her stunning red and gold silk sari that Swami blessed years ago. Craig was dressed in a new suit, complete with shoes, shirt, and tie, borrowed from Vijay, who wore the exact same size. When Swami came by, he blessed Craig's head and both wedding rings, announcing His joy with a "Very happy, very happy" emotional sigh!

The Wedding Mass was to begin at 12 noon. Some of their friends had expressed their regrets because they were lead bhajan singers and Sunday bhajans were sung all day, so they would not be able to leave the ashram. It seemed as if Sai accommodated them too, because He concluded bhajans at ten, and now all their friends could attend the wedding. The devotees left in a hurry to decorate the church with flowers.

The church bells rang and the choir sang as the maid-of-honor, flower girls, father, and bride marched down the red-carpeted aisle. All the devotees who came to celebrate their wedding day with them, each contributed in some sweet way.

Someone gave the wedding bouquet, someone the flowers, someone the video, and someone even gave the bride away. The photographer gave his time, took pictures, and developed the video. They had no money to pay, so God provided the way. The reception, a gift so grand was held in an elegant manner, in fact the Windsor Manor a luxurious hotel in Bangalore. Hugs and good wishes were exchanged as each guest passed by the bride and groom. The banquet table was laden with treats - all veggies, no meats. It was a day always to remember.

After a few days honeymoon in Madras, Craig and Patricia flew home to visit her family, who now lived in Edmonton, Canada. Robert and I drove to Canada to meet our new family. There was so much joy in having in-laws who are devotees. We all sat together, thanking Our Lord Sai as we watched the Wedding Ceremony on video.

Our eyes could hardly believe the grandeur and beauty! Baba's love and grace far exceeded ours. The more we "let go," the higher his love soars!

Truth is what I teach
Righteousness is what I do
Peace is what I am
Love is My Self

You are Mine and I am yours.

BABA

VERANDA

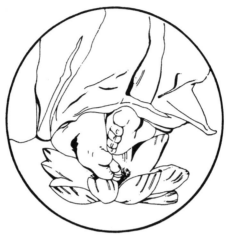

There was great joy in our hearts in December 1986. The recently-wed couple, our son Craig and Patricia and both sets of parents, the Narinesingh's and Bruce's visited Sai Baba, for the first time as a family, at this auspicious season, when we celebrate the birth of Jesus Christ.

The week before we were to leave for Prasanthi Nilayam on our seventh journey to our Lord, my thoughts frequently dwelt on our trip to see Sai Baba. 'What will this trip teach us? Will we get a family interview?' It would give us great joy to share an interview with our children and in-laws. Robert and I had some unanswered questions, and we were seeking direction from Baba. Our youngest daughter had a proposal for marriage and had been asking Sai Baba for His blessings and approval. Robert's position at work could call for a change of location, and I needed to know if Swami really wanted me to write. These questions sought answers; but as the days became nearer to leaving, I again questioned my motives for wanting an interview.

"When devotees surrender their lives to God and obey Him, He takes the full responsibility and cares for His devotees even to the smallest details." We had seen this principle work in our lives countless times, and if the questions do not get answered by Baba personally on the outer level, He will guide us to His will, through the inner level voice, and the circumstances of our life.

The weeks at Prashanti disappeared quickly, even though we had wonderful darshan, and the blessings of being with our Lord sharing His Divine Presence with our own family members. There had been no invitation for an interview.

The day arrived when all the family must leave for home except for Robert and myself. We had an extra week. I waved them farewell with mixed emotions longing for the interview and yet with much gratitude for the trip and all the darshan attention. In the first week of our stay in Prasanthi, I had awakened with the message, "No interview for you this trip." The last time I heard that message, it was indeed correct. So this time I really believed there would be no interview.

Next morning at, darshan, Sai Baba told Robert to "Go" for an interview. As I saw Robert walking towards the veranda, I felt disbelief. It was the first time I had that reaction. I also got up, and walked to the veranda very happy but puzzled. Swami had said no interview!

and why did He call us now after the family was gone? "Who can understand the ways of the Lord?" I thought.

Swami called the ladies into the interview room, and as I approached Him, I thanked Him for the interview. He took my hands and in a gentle but firm manner said, *"I'll see you later."* I was stunned and started to sit back down, but Mataji the lady Seva Dal on duty on the veranda said to me "'later' can mean tomorrow or any time," and ushered me away from the verandah. I was in shock . . . His words kept echoing through my mind, *"I'll see you later."*

It was the most difficult walk of my life. I realized that I was receiving the same karma that I had caused for Catherine on our wedding day. I asked Sai within, "What are you trying to tell me?" To get so close to an interview and be turned away with such a deliberate action must have a definite reason. I could feel the crushing blow of Sai's hammer on my ego. Within moments, I was experiencing the emotional pull of the two opposites, first the joy of going for an interview and then the pain of rejection. How our emotions swing back and forth, like a monkey from tree to tree, chasing after desires. I felt tears beginning to swell in my eyes, and a turbulent storm of emotions brewing within. My eyes darted about, looking for an inconspicuous place to sit. Uncontrolled emotions, displayed publicly are not the ideal way to get Swami's attention or approval.

As I sat across from the interview room, I used my intellect to calm my stormy feelings. I remembered Sai's teachings. *"In order to become free from the twin pulls*

272

of pleasure and pain, one must rid oneself of the body-consciousness, and keep clear of self-centered actions. " I kept repeating, "I am God; not the body. Maintain your equilibrium, do not respond to this action. Be detached." Such lofty advice was coming from inside the one who felt so human and rejected. It was His miracle that allowed me to stay calm, enough to keep me from bursting into tears. I was grateful and surprised that there was some measure of control.

Sai says, *"For the Voice of God is to be heard in the region of your heart only when the tongue is stilled, and the storm is stilled, and the waves are calm."* So I silenced myself inside and again asked "What have I done wrong . . . what are you telling me?" I heard His reply. "Two years ago in meditation I told you to write a book, but for the past six months you have stopped. You are spending too much time with your family. I have told you to detach from your husband and have a spiritual marriage. You are eating too much, wasting time and energy, and spending too much money. What has happened to my ceiling on desires' program?" I could immediately see how I had failed him.

"Oh, Baba, you are so right." The pain stuck in my heart. I conversed with Him inside. "Many times I have rejected you by putting husband, family, and sense pleasures before you. I have become "spiritually sloppy" these past six months. Oh, Baba, I am sorry for offending you." I felt so guilty and sad.

"Embodiments of love! Do not feel bad because Swami has told you things harshly. In fact, a true guru (great spiritual teacher) is harsh when it is necessary.

273

Beware of the treacherous fellow who tries to deceive you by hiding your defects." I began to realize He had personally given me the priceless gift of learning and growing, through His experience. I began to look at more of the details.

Sai Baba initiated a program called "Ceiling on Desires" several years before his 60th birthday celebration. He said, That if we wanted to give Him a gift for His birthday, it should be one of lessening our desires. He classified our desires in four categories: food, money, energy, and time. *"One thing that is harming us and our countries is laziness. By being lazy, we are being treacherous to our own country and our own community. We must control our desires. Put a ceiling on desires.*

"The first rule is: Do not waste money. The misuse of money is evil. A lot of money is being wasted on unnecessary travel and other unnecessary things.

"The second rule is: Don't waste time. Time is God. Time wasted is life wasted. By wasting time, we are wasting our divinity, our divine power.

"The third rule is: Don't waste food. And the fourth rule is: Don't waste energy. Western people waste all four of these things. They waste money, they waste time, they waste food, and they waste energy. Because of the waste of these, all of life is wasted. Life is a valuable thing. Life is full of divinity. But we are spending all of our time looking at the external world."

When Swami told me to leave the veranda, I could feel his power and strength. As I sat outside waiting for the interview to end, I recalled my experience. I'm not sure how it happened, but I felt that Sai transferred some of His energy to me. I knew that He had equipped me with the necessary discipline to achieve His goals.

I also realized the mercy of His Divine timing, Swami called Robert for an interview without me on the day following the family's departure. To experience that on my own was severe; with my family watching, their concern for me would have intensified my pain. Even our disappointments are His grace, if we only STOP, LOOK, & LISTEN, I reminded myself.

The interview door opened, and I saw a beautiful smile on Robert's face. I was so relieved to see his glowing face. As we walked to our room, he comforted me. "Don't worry, Rita, everything is allright. I have some news from Swami for you and it will make you very happy. When we get to the room, I'll tell you everything."

Robert shared his interview, and I shared the inner-view. Swami gave Robert the same messages inside His room as He had given me outside. Sai Baba again confirmed to me that the voice I hear is His. There will be no mistaking His instructions this time, nor in the future.

Baba wanted us to have a spiritual marriage. We had spent our entire life together developing a close, more loving relationship. Now that we had our desire fulfilled, we must detach from it. We met when I was sixteen, and we had created a network of attachments.

Robert and I needed to cut the ties that bind us to each other, and instead bind ourselves closer to God.

Even Swami's actions on the veranda were a sign. He physically separated us. His action was telling us that we each must find God alone. Each of us had our own individual spiritual destiny.

Since our spiritual wedding day, April 17, 1983, Baba had given us some firm clues. Twice during that trip, he told Robert, *"Don't touch."* On our trip in 1985, again on the veranda, waiting for an interview, Swami asked me, *"Where is your husband?"* I pointed to Robert. He looked into my eyes and said, *"Husband or has-been husband?"* Baba speaks only a few words, but conveys paragraphs! Again he emphasised our spiritual union.

In his interview that morning, Robert asked Baba, "What should my wife do about her writing?" Sai looked at him with great seriousness and firmly stated, *"Your wife should write,"* and then his voice changed into sweetness, *"I will bless her."*

Five years ago, during an hour of silence at our Central Regional Conference, Sai Baba told me to write a book about my experiences as a devotee. He said to write about His teachings and how they have changed my life. The mind started its game of denial. It told me, "It must be a joke. You can't write. How can you write a book, when you've never written? And you haven't read that much either!" Had I imagined this instruction to write I wondered? In this case desire was not the culprit – fear was. Fear and desire weaken our actions, and our capacity to act.

I began writing and found it almost impossible. I would write and rewrite. It was a workout only, I was 'pumping intellectual and spiritual iron!' Writing was a lesson in discipline, patience and perseverance. These were the same virtues I had expanded when I was ill. If that illness had not occurred, I question if I could have sat long enough to write, much less have the patience. Even then I was still uncertain of the authenticity of my message.

In our 1986 trip to India I wrote a yes/no note to Baba to confirm that message given in meditation. During darshan, Swami was not walking close to where I was sitting, but He saw my note and deliberately came over and took it. So the answer was "Yes". I wrote a few articles, and they were published in some of the Sai publications. I felt that it was Baba's method of encouraging me. It was not easy to learn a new skill, it took me much effort. It seems that the older we become, the more we resist change, but basically I think the resistance is better described as laziness. It takes energy to learn new skills or change a behavior. The older we become, the less energy we have. It's easier to stay as we are and not change.

At last, I plunged into writing a book, struggling, but improving slowly. I continually said, "Sai, you are the Doer, not I. I am the instrument." It took months, but I was making some progress. When Craig and Patricia came home from India in May 1986, to live with us, I stopped writing. I became so involved with the family that I had "no time" for writing. I had found my excuse not to do it.

"When you are given some work, you should put your heart and soul into it and do the work with the utmost

sincerity and dedication to the limit of your capacity. Take, for example, a person who is entrusted with planting trees and developing a garden. If he does the work wholeheartedly, the plants will come up well and the garden will grow into a thing of beauty. When Swami comes to see that garden and feels happy with the condition of the plants, then Swami's joy becomes the grace he bestows on that person, and that Grace will confer great happiness on that individual."

The mind is tricky. It likes to justify its behavior. I justified mine with the excuse of uncertainty.

Messages that come from the inner-voice are so subtle that we like to ignore them or discredit them as invalid especially if they are inconvenient to our current way of life, and require real effort.

Baba's little parable on the veranda, "husband or has been husband," could also be justified as God's funny little joke, and His words could be ignored. But 'has been husband' means Robert is my husband, and I will serve Him as a dutiful wife but he was no longer to be thought of **mentally** as my husband. Mentally my thoughts belong to God.

Recounting my mistakes may help some readers to avoid making errors in the future, and it helps me to remember not to repeat a worn-out behavior pattern. I have learned that Sai Baba gives us subtle hints, and His jokes are often very serious. No word He utters to us is in vain, He is conveying a message. It's up to us to understand and implement His message. He's very fair. He gave me two warnings, the inner message at the retreat and His accepting my yes/no note in darshan, both said I was to write. The third time He took action. Believe me, He got His message across the third time. This is the same method we can use on our children, to teach them right conduct.

It was time for me to look at my fear of writing. Fear can run so deep and silent, like a submarine, that it's hard to recognize from the surface, yet it is there but it can threaten and weaken the security of all our feelings.

I had always felt intellectually insecure from old programming. "I'm just a housewife" – I would say, you know the saying. The first intellectual put-down I can remember was in high school. My literature teacher told me that I would never be good for anything other than marriage. Her remarks torpedoed my intellectual self-image submarine, and it submerged a little. Over the years continual intellectual rejection finally sank that submarine with a hull full of fear. It could no longer float. At this stage of my development it was time to bring up the old wreck with its sunken treasure and free it to float again. Spiritual growth is achieved by cleansing our inner-self from fears, prejudices, desires, and hatred.

"Ego is what prevents you from getting close to God. You are embodiments of the divine atma. Do not crave for recognition and respect from others; crave rather for winning grace from the Lord."

Sai says, *"The six enemies of man are eating into his vitals, embedded in his own inner consciousness. They are the demons to be killed. They are lust, anger, greed, attachment, pride, and malice."* It takes energy to hold these negative enemies in our subconscious. Once released, the energy is free for use in developing higher consciousness. The more garbage we dump, the lighter we are for spiritual travel.

I failed to have complete faith in my inner voice, because fear and desire weakened my trust in the intuitive nature of God's voice within. Was the voice speaking to me from the sense of I or the sense of we are God.

The ego wants temporary pleasure and tempts the senses. Our desire for pleasure drowns out the still soft voice of God. Our ego is so strong that the message of the inner voice can only be heard in the lull, or quiet times between the bombardment of countless desires in our minds. Meditation is an attempt to create a lull and a quiet space in which to hear or listen to 'the still small voice'.

We have all experienced talking with a chatterbox, and how difficult it is to speak one word, much less a sentence. The chatterbox only wants one-way communication, and is not interested or aware that you have anything to contribute. The same analogy can be applied to our "ego chatterbox" and the voice of God. If you are mathematical, you can put this in equation form: Strong desire = less God; Less desire = more God.

The voice of the atma gets stronger and clearer as the ego begins to learn its <u>primary</u> function, to turn inward to receive instructions for all action from God.

"No activity should be taken up with individual aggrandizement in view; intellect and emotion must be directed to the revelation of the resident in the heart, atma; every act should be done sincerely, with love, with no yearning for acquiring personal profit, fame, or benefit. Above all, listen to the voice of God within. As soon as one contemplates a wrong act, that voice warns, protests, and advises giving up."....."The present is a product of the past, but it is also the seed for the future."

The more we practice listening and trusting the voice of God, the more confident we become. He is an excellent teacher and has helped me to cast away some of the shadows and doubts. His message to me is clear. Trust your inner voice and act accordingly. When I learn from my past mistakes and apply the knowledge that He has taught, then my future will bear fruit for God.

Robert communicated his entire interview to me slowly. I wanted to savor every detail. Sai had given approval of a marriage partner for our youngest daughter Joan. She was nine when we first heard about Sai Baba, and she has been critical of Baba throughout the years. Ever since her brother, Craig, whom she admires, went to India and openly professed his devotion to Sai Baba, Joan seemed to be a little more receptive.

Before we departed for India, she came to me with a picture of her boyfriend and herself, asking if I would bring it to Sai for His approval of marriage. I was completely taken by surprise, but delighted. It was a positive step in the right direction. It looked like Sai was dangling His hook near Joan.

I remembered her outburst when I told her that Sai Baba brought Craig and Patricia together for marriage. "How can he marry her after only knowing her a few months," she asked? "How can he possibly know her? Craig must be crazy. She is an Indian girl, her culture is so different from ours. How will she fit in with Craig's friends? I can't believe he is doing this." She was afraid for her brother.

I simply replied, "I trust your brother's judgment. But the most significant fact to remember in this marriage arrangement, Joan, is that Sai Baba is God. If Sai approves of their marriage, then it will be absolutely correct for their spiritual growth. Joan, you can't go any higher than God for approval."

Joan was anxious to meet her new sister Patricia. At first, she accepted her formally, but somewhere between welcome... . . to our . . . family, they became good friends. I'm certain that Joan was motivated to seek Sai's advice because of the compatibility she saw between Craig and Patricia.

Throughout the day, Sai Baba kept sending devotees to our door. But as night fell, after evening darshan, I felt the strain of today's event. I couldn't control the tears any longer. Swami's rejection was more than I could handle. Human rejection will never have the same effect it had on me in the past. God's rejection is the only rejection we should be concerned about.

Looking back, I realize that Sai showed and taught us something of the wonder of His Omnipresence. He took Robert inside the interview room and gave him messages in spoken words and gestures. He left me outside in the darshan line and gave me the same messages through my inner view. Our mutual sharing, trust and love enabled us to perceive and experience his One-ness.

PRASANTHI NILAYAM

DIVINE DISCOURSE

*A*t *Prasanthi Nilayam, every day is a Festival Day; every day is a holy day. As the saying goes, it is – "Perpetual joy, Perpetually green."*

This Nilayam (abode) is "Prasanthi" Nilayam. It is the abode of the highest form of Santhi, Prasanthi. In fact, you are, each one of you, the Nilayam of Prasanthi. That is why I very often address you as 'Santhiswarupulaara!' My object is to remind you that your real nature is Santhi, equanimity, peace, unruffledness, non-attachment. You cannot draw out from within you that which is not there, can you ? Therefore, Peace must be there, deep down, as the very core of your being. It is the ripeness of the fruit, the sweetness filling the ripened fruit.

This Prasanthi Nilayam has no compound wall, as you have noticed. It is, as it should be; people can come to the Lord from any direction, without let or hindrance. But we have gates! The persons who walk along the road, which takes a turn when it approaches the Nilayam are, like all else, burdened with inherited impulses and earned dents and bends in their personality make-up. They are moved on by desire and urged by the six-pronged whip of passion. They enter the gate only when they are no longer overwhelmed by Thamoguna; that is, when they have the curtain of delusion drawn aside a little. From there they move on towards the Nilayam and pass through that second gate, where they are attracted by the imposing building, the portico, the statue infront all appealing to the comparatively superior quality of Passion. Even this falls off when they enter the Hall, where the Pure quality overpowers the mind what with the pictures, images, the Bhajana, the Namavalis (String of names) etc.

Prasanthi Nilayam is the spiritually uplifting center for the whole world; Devotees from all over the world are here, so the slightest mistake or wrong committed by you will be the talk of the world. Your behavior must be exemplary; every country must learn lessons from you. The foundation must not give way; you must be strong and steady, sincere and straight. Nor should you suffer from conceit, that you have been chosen to exercise authority over others.

People of all ages, of all states of health and wealth, of various levels of learning and intelligence come to Prasanthi Nilayam. This Prasanthi Nilayam is also the refuge for all who have no other place to go to. Do not treat anyone as an alien. Remember all have Me as their guardian and support. Have no anger, malice, envy or pride against or before anyone. Be full of humility; have faith in human goodness.

As a matter of fact, the world itself is fundamentally a Prasanthi Nilayam. I want each of you to so transform yourself during this period that you will carry with you the atmosphere of the Prasanthi Nilayam wherever you go, for, you cannot live happily in any surrounding that is not fragrant with love and humility, discipline and control. You will naturally endeavor to make this place where you are and the men among whom you move, a bit more spiritual than before.

This Nilayam should not be treated with scant reverence. Make the best use of your stay here. Do not treat this chance lightly. You come spending much money, and put yourselves to much trouble to reach here; but, you do not bloom as fragrant offerings at the Lord's Feet by learning the Spiritual path. The senses have to be curbed into obedient servants of the spirit.

For example, I insist on Silence. Talk less, talk low when you must talk. Do not thrust your sorrows, your needs, your problems into the ears of those who have come here with their own bundle of such things. They are to listen to you, to console you. Do not by loudness of voice disturb those who are meditating or reading or writing the Name of God.

Meditate if possible, by yourselves, alone; read spiritual books if you can; write the Name of the Lord in the quiet of

286

your corner; if you cannot do these, at least do not disturb others who are doing these. Encourage one another to march along the Path of God.

You may be in this Prasanthi Nilayam area but, if you worry more about physical needs and comforts than Prayer beads and Meditation your stay is a waste. You have made no progress at all. The waving of the camphor flame at the end of the Bhajans session is to remind you that your sensual cravings must be burnt away, without leaving any trace behind, and you must offer your self to God as beings merged with His Glory.

In this Prasanthi Nilayam, too, there are certain limits laid down, certain modes of spending time usefully, recommended by Me. All who come here, whether long-time residents or new arrivals, have to observe them. You have seen Me, and stayed here, and heard these Discourses. Let Me ask what is the gain? Are you going back, unchanged, unaffected? Dogs do not gnaw sugar cane; they seek a bone, instead. Ill-fated mortals recoil, when the talk is about goodness, Spiritual discipline and Self Realization.

But you must pull yourselves up into the purer air of Spiritual life, draw yourselves away from slums and by-lanes and travel on the highway to God. Dwell always on the glory of God; then you will shine in that Glory. Adhere to Truth, that is the surest means of removing fear from your heart. Love can grow only in the heart watered by Truth.

There are people, at the Nilayam, who have been here for twenty, fifteen, and ten years and such long periods, but

287

only their bodies have grown older; their yearning, to do seva (service) has not grown. Life at the Prasanthi Nilayam may deepen faith in the Seva path to salvation. It is the attitude that is essential. The particular item of service might be small. You may not get a chance to partake in some gigantic scheme of service through which millions maybe benefited; you can lift a lame lamb over a stile, or lead a blind child across a busy road. Doing voluntary service at the Nilayam, is also an act of worship.

Do not pretend or patronize. If you simply say "Do not talk aloud" or give some such blank direction, you are patronizing and treating people with disdain. They deserve to be told why. Tell them that silence is the very first rung of the ladder of Spiritual discipline; that is the hall mark of Prasanthi Nilayam; that they must learn to make every place where they are, a Prasanthi Nilayam; the loud talk disturbs those who practice the Repetition of the name of God or Meditation or Prayer beads. Such noise breeds further noise.

Do not cultivate too much attachment to things of the world, which appeal to carnal desires and several thirsts. A moment comes when you have to depart empty-handed, leaving all that you have laboriously collected and proudly called your own. Persons who live in the Prasanthi Nilayam as well as those who come here for short stay have dozens of bags, boxes and bundles, vessels of various sizes in plenty, in fact, a truck load of pots and pans; but look at the American Devotees who are here. They have come across the oceans or the continents, thousands of miles with a bag, a rug and a can. You spend most of your time worrying about the goods you pile around yourself.

I am insisting on five points of discipline for the permanent residents of Prasanthi Nilayam. I shall tell you about them, for your homes and your villages have to be transformed into Prasanthi Nilayam. They are:

1. Silence. This is the first step in spiritual discipline, it makes the other steps easy. It promotes self-control; it lessens chances of anger, hate, malice, greed and pride. Besides, you can hear His Footsteps, only when silence reigns in the mind.

2. Cleanliness: It is the doorway to Godliness. Inner and outer cleanliness are essential, if you desire to install God in your heart.

3. Service: Service saves you from the agony you get when another suffers; it broadens your vision, widens your awareness, deepens your compassion. All waves are on the same sea, from the same sea, merge in the same sea. Seva teaches you to be firm in this knowledge.

4. Love: Do not cultivate or weigh the reaction, result or reward. Love calls; Love responds. Love is God, Live in Love.

5. Hatelessness. No being is to be looked down upon as secondary, inferior, unimportant or expendable. Each has its allotted role in the drama designed by the Almighty. Do not slight, insult or injure any being; for He is in every being and your slight becomes a sacrilege.

Some feel that the disciplines of the Prasanthi Nilayam are limited to the geographical bounds of this area and so they can be ignored when one is beyond the gates.

The whole world must appear as a Prasanthi Nilayam, not simply, this stone and cement structure. As a matter of fact, the world is fundamentally, a Prasanthi Nilayam; only man by his ignorance and perversity has fouled it into a snake-pit of crime and hate.

This is the reason why we have certain disciplines at the Prasanthi Nilayam, which you are all expected to follow. Maintaining silence as a step in spiritual discipline which you learn here and practice wherever you go is the most potent of these rules. You are advised to spend time in meditation or prayer beads or the quiet pursuit of the Repetition of God's name; for peace and joy are not to be found in external nature; they are treasures lying hidden in the inner realms of man; once they are located, man can never more be sad or agitated.

Study well the disciplinary rules laid down for all who wish to be in Prasanthi Nilayam. These rules are for your own good. Wherever you are, you can make the place a Prasanthi Nilayam. Become sharers in My History. Do not go far from Me. You have acquired nearness through the accumulated good fortune of many births. It you cut this contact and get away, a time will come when you will weep outside the gates clamoring for entry. Be free from silly delusions and doubts, be free from tawdry desires–and I shall take you into Me.

Into this Prasanthi Nilayam, persons come from all parts of the world, at all stages of development, with all types of problems, afflicted with all forms of pain or grief, inspired with all varieties of promptings. This is a workshop where damaged minds and hearts come for repair or overhaul. In most workshops, there will be the din of hammer, the clang of wheel, the whir of engine and the clatter of chains. In this workshop, there must be heard only the whisper of the Name of the God. With new parts fitted and new coats of paint, cars emerge out of the workshop as good as new and they run smoothly, without trouble, for miles and miles. People should find this place also to be a workshop for persons, who are travel-worn, weary, or about to enter upon a long journey.

So use this holy atmosphere, this splendid chance, these precious days to the fullest. With every inhalation, utter the name of God with every exhalation utter the name of God. Live in God, for Him, with Him.

There is a popular tune in Telugu, "Brindavan is everyone's, Govinda belongs to all." Similarly, Prasanthi Nilayam belongs to every one, Baba belongs to all.

- SATHYA SAI BABA

JOURNEY HOME

It was my good-by darshan. I sat in one of the back rows as He walked past, ignoring my presence. Inside, I whispered, "Please look my way." I hear Him say, "No, it's better this way." I felt the flood gate lift and the tear control alarm sounded. I wanted to cry, but instead I detached. Sai says, *"Detachment is sacrifice."*

We finished our last-minute packing and started down the stairs. Phyllis Krystal was standing there. I said, "Phyllis, for the last two days I have had the feeling that Sai Baba wants us to go for a reading from the Book of Bhrighu. I was told that you have the address. Before I went to sleep last night, I asked Sai if He wants us to go, please send us Phyllis before we leave. And here you are!"

We went to her room to get the address. She remarked

that this is the first time in several trips that she had brought the address with her and had had several requests for it.

Since I knew very little about the readings, I asked her to explain. It appears there was a sage named Bhrighu who lived 5000 years ago. While in a trance, he received this knowledge foretelling the destiny of some people. He wrote it on thousands of palm leaves. The Book does not contain everyone's name, only those who are destined to come for a reading, to the priest who keeps the book.

The day and time you come are your destiny times. Supposedly, no-one will feel the need to go until it is their time. The pundit measures the length of your shadow in the sunlight. The length of your shadow, birth date, destiny time, all calculated together determine which palm leaf reading is yours.

"Is it accurate," I asked?

Phyllis said "I took notes at first, but the reading predicted so many outstanding experiences with Sai Baba and also said I would write some books. You see I had not even met Sai Baba then. I was so disappointed in myself for going to see this fortune - teller. I couldn't believe a word he predicted. But that was fourteen years ago, and since that time, the readings have come true!

"I asked Sai Baba if the Book of Brighu writings are accurate. Baba said that the palm leaves were accurate, but the true meaning can be lost through the translation." I wrote down the address, although she was uncertain if he still lives in that residence. She told me that the pundit speaks no English, so I will need an English translator to accompany us.

I was grateful for her explanation and help, and I thanked her as we walked to the entrance of the round building where we stayed. I was surprised to see so many dear friends gathered on the porch. "It seems as though Sai has sent you a "good-by" committee," said Catherine. In my previous trips, Sai had always given me a personal good-by. This trip it was denied, but He extended His grace and sent His loving devotees.

Another farewell to God's earthly home. With each trip to Baba, one never knows ahead of time what to expect, what challenges and lessons He will place before you. We never know what will happen. But from experience, I knew that there would be a change in my consciousness by the time I departed. Each time I left, I felt as if my emotional car had had mechanical adjustments, some times more extensively than others. I wondered which fender I had left behind this time.

As we passed through the gate leaving Prasanthi, I still felt shaken from the trauma of the last part of this trip. But I knew that somehow between leaving and arriving back home I would begin to experience the new model car rolling off the assembly line. After so many trips, I was familiar with the pattern. It's definitely Sai's repair shop; the place where we drop off old unwanted parts and get shiny new ones.

"Prasanthi Nilayam is the spiritual uplifting center for the whole world. It is the refuge for all who have no other place to go. It is a workshop where damaged minds and

hearts come for repair or overhaul." Sai's words echoed in my mind.

Years ago, through inner communication, I had an explanation describing God's method for changing our consciousness. It has helped me to understand the process. I was told that "to change consciousness, God first needs to open our consciousness. This is usually accomplished by some emotional crisis. The strength of the crisis determines the size of the opening, and that subsequently influences the amount of change."

My inner voice continued. "It's an internal earthquake, and that is the reason why you feel so shaken. Once the consciousness is open, it makes room for expanded consciousness by removing old programs of thought, feelings and the consequent behavior fills the space with the Oneness of Atmic Vision. This wisdom changes behavior and adds strength to the existing foundation.

"A foundation must be strong and unshakable before the structure can rise. Once floors are added to the structure, that is the higher consciousness, external influences such as earthquakes, (emotional storms) must not penetrate the building in that way you can witness the events of daily living without responding violently to them."

I was told, "Visualize a crack made by an earthquake. This crack is filled with new earth. The original closure will never return; therefore, what exists is a new expansion of the surface–expanded consciousness, in man."

So, why do I go to India to see Sai Baba? Why do I travel so far, suffer physical inconvenience, exhaustion, and often illness plus the emotional and mental stress? I go for expansion of my consciousness, for Love.

The real miracle of Prasanthi Nilayam materializes, as we live with Sai Baba in His energy field of love. His Love energy transforms us, and expands our ability to give and receive Love. As He performs spiritual surgery, He wraps His energy field of love around us and He absorbs the shock of the quake. This eases our karma...we call it Grace.

"Expansion is life. Expansion is the essence of love. Love is God. Live in love.

"Love can transform man into a divine being; it helps him to manifest the divine which is his core.

"God is the source of all love. Love God, love the world as the vesture of God, no more no less. Through love you can merge in the ocean of love. Love cures pettiness, hate, and grief. Love loosens bonds. It saves man from the torment of birth and death. Love binds all hearts in a soft silken symphony. Seen through the eyes of love, all beings are beautiful, all deeds are dedicated, all thoughts are innocent, the world is one vast family."

Our plane landed late in Bombay, and we had an hour's drive to the President Hotel. We only had one day in Bombay; we were due to depart the next night. The first item on our agenda was to call for an appointment with Mr. Kantilal Pandya, the pundit who reads the Book of Brighu. We had his address, but no phone number. The Krystals felt certain that someone at the hotel would know of him.

We asked the manager, who checked with the staff and telephone book, but found nothing. We were told to contact a Mr. Ravi at 8:00 a.m. because he would know where to inquire. Before sleeping, we again called upon Sai, "If it's Your Will, please help us to find this pundit."

Robert returned to the lobby at 8:00 a.m. seeking Mr. Ravi, but he had not come to work today. Robert was told to see the business manager at 9:00 a.m. We continued our inquiry because one must never give up too soon, especially in India.

Behind the business manager's desk sat a very sweet young lady who ended our search. She had never heard of Mr. Pandya, but referred to the phone book, even though I stated that the manager had looked last night. She said, "I prefer to recheck."

Thank Sai! There was the name, address, and phone number of the pundit. She could speak Hindi and placed the call. It seemed that Mr. Pandya can speak English and no translator was necessary. He had taken English lessons. How fortunate for us because a second translator lessens the accuracy. He would be available to see us at 10:00 a.m. She wrote out directions for the taxi driver. The address was only fifteen minutes ride from our hotel.

We introduced ourselves and immediately were taken out into the sun for our shadow measurement. We gave him our birth date. He calculated and then brought forth some palm leaves wrapped in a protective covering.

I had heard of the Book of Brighu ten years ago, but

297

had never had any desire to get a reading until two days before we left Prasanthi. How strange? It defied logic, but there we were on January 17, 1987, waiting to hear our reading.

We each had separate readings. Since Robert and I have mutually shared so many experiences our readings were somewhat similar. We were both told that Sathya Sai Baba would be our spiritual teacher in this life. Baba would give us rings and a photo of Him with us, and give me a medallion. We would travel to India many times, and Baba will see us and talk with us many times. Thus far what was read was true.

He said that Robert and I were born in India and were husband and wife in our last lifetime. We were both devotees of Shirdi Sai. This lifetime, we were both born in America because of our death wish to see America. Our next life will be spent in India, both males, Brahmacharya, living at Prema Sai's ashram. We will be good friends and come to the ashram at a very young age and spend our entire life with Prema Sai.

He continued, "Sai Baba will tell you, only it's more like a command to start writing NOW!"

I questioned him. "Is this statement written in the palm leaves?"

"Yes," he replied.

"Is the word NOW written?" I inquired.

"Yes," said the pundit.

I could hardly believe what I was hearing. The memory of our interview experience, so fresh that I still trembled with its impact, and this was written 5,000 years ago on palm leaves? Incredible!

The word NOW referred to our present trip. If we had decided to come during any other trip, the statement would have been invalid. The three-letter word "now" certainly substantiated the theory that you are destined to arrive at a fixed time. The balance of the reading was about our spiritual life.

It's hard to believe that this was written 5,000 years ago, predetermined. I must admit that this experience did stun me, because suddenly my whole life flashed before me looking at the events from a much different perspective. How many times I thought: I am the doer, I am in control, I have done this and that in my life? The ego is so strong and wants the ultimate control.

This new experience enlarged my vision of God as the doer and my relationship to Him. Sometimes we know the Truth but when it is experienced it becomes Wisdom and because this event with Sai Baba was so intense and emotional, the force of these feelings embedded permanently in my consciousness this Truth, that God is the doer; I am only an instrument.

"Man has two eyes; he sees only past and present. God has three eyes. God's eyes are spiritual. He sees in front, behind, above, below...God is the present. He is Omnipresent. As Baba looks at people, He sees the past, the present moment, and the future and everywhere in every direction."

Is God determining my future? I hope so. Baba tells us if we choose to turn to the world, to follow our own ego desires, then we are free to work out our own destiny. If we choose to surrender to God, He will protect, guide, and provide even beyond our requests.

In 1984, Dr. Hislop asked Baba, "One has the free will to choose to turn to God or to be fully involved with the world. But on the other hand, when Baba looks at a person, at one glance He sees, the past, present, and future of that person, so how can there be free will?"

Baba replied, *"From that viewpoint, of the Divine, there is no free will, for all is God. But from the ego viewpoint of the individual there is free will. There is general law, (Gods Law) and then the individual and society. The individual acts in society according to his free will, but all conform to the general law. The individual must act and his action is a function of his mind. There are thoughts. Thoughts are seeds. They sprout and become actions. The actions then appear to be free will to the concerned individual. Everyone has been given skills and talents such as intelligence, reason, energy, and they must be put into life action."*

It is easier for me to understand if I view the world as a classroom with Baba as the teacher, and I the student. For example, imagine I am in the sixth grade. My teacher has already planned the course that he will teach me this year. He knows the material he will teach day by day. My responsibility as a student is to observe, work, and learn. It is the same in the classroom of life. God knows the grade and year of study we're in and determines the necessary lessons for "our personal journey to God."

If with my own free-will, I surrender my ego to God, then there is no separation–God and I are the same person. So God, a part of me, selects a role for me to perform in His play. He has set the stage and written the script for me. As I live through this role, I learn from these experiences. Sai tells us to experience. Why?

Because when we have **"VISION OF SAI"** we will know our identity is Divine and finally "ARRIVE HOME."

ABOUT THE AUTHOR

Rita Bruce has been a Sai Baba devotee for 19 years. In that time, she has traveled to India to study eighteen times and has attended 70 classes. She says that "living with Sai Baba and His teachings is not easy, but he is teaching me to have inner strength, to fight the war of good over evil, to fail and to understand my failing, to struggle with the ills of society and the results that have scarred my soul so that—in the end—I can reach my goals." She is the author of *Vision of Sai—Book 2*, also published by Samuel Weiser.

She currently lives in Tucson, Arizona.